The Longfellah's Son

An Almost True Irish Story

By
Michael Cassidy

Michael Cassidy Publications

Audio Production by Pro Audio Voices
www.proaudiovoices.com

ISBN-13: 978-0-9987606-0-5

Cover Design by Andy Parker
www.andyparkerdesign.com

Available in audio (read by the author), print and ebook editions.

DEDICATION
This book is dedicated to my son Brian with regret at a
childhood denied,
but with joy at the man you have become.

ACKNOWLEDGEMENTS

With thanks to bestselling author Adair Lara for your encouragement when this project began fifteen years ago. Without you Adair, I would never have written this book.

Special thanks to my editor Jil Plummer for your contribution over many years. Your direction, endless patience and editorial skills were invaluable. I will never be able to sufficiently thank you.

Thanks also to my audiobook producer, Becky Parker Geist of Pro Audio Voices, another talented professional who helped me get this book across the finish line.

Thanks to my Irish heritage for giving me a love of language and the stubbornness to complete this project.

Thanks to my parents who loved me as best they could.

Thanks to my wonderful, big sister. Your little brother loves and misses you.

Thanks most of all to Brian for your understanding and forgiveness.

Table of Contents

Longfellah's Son

Chapter One

EXILE

There was one final task to face before leaving. Since sobering up, Murphy saw his son Brian's face in every young boy he'd see. The harm he'd done to the innocent child remained a continuous ache in his heart. But now he was going to increase the damage by leaving Ireland, putting the distance of an ocean and a continent between them.

Brian had turned five the week before. His father's visit would be a questionable, belated birthday present. That surprisingly warm March afternoon saw a swirling haze floating on the surface of the river Lee as it drifted lazily beside the Marina. He'd spent time wondering how he could explain why he was leaving for America but gave up in frustration. There was no satisfactory explanation. Telling the child he was unemployable, was finished in Ireland, would make no sense at his age.

He'd occasionally seen him over the previous year. The first time was when his mother brought him to the shopping center in Douglas. He'd taken the bus up from Limerick terrified all the way that it might break down and he'd miss the appointment. The boy's mother would drop him off, he could have him for three hours then was to return him to their new home but not come inside the door. She was renting a house in Carrigaline barely a stone's throw from their home he'd caused to be repossessed. She was now living with another man Murphy had introduced her to when he was reaching rock bottom. There was a degree of sad consolation they were together since he knew he could never take care of them, but Billy could. He was a good man who'd become Brian's real father.

On that fateful day, one year before, a handsome four-year-old boy dressed in brown pants, brown sweater, check shirt, and shining brown shoes had stood before him, eyes downward. His light blond hair had a fringe falling delicately over his forehead. His eyes lake blue. He offered a shy, gentle smile before looking quickly away. He barely knew who the man hovering silently above him was. Had only vague memories of him. Both were painfully nervous.

Soon they were sitting in the restaurant of the Metropole hotel cautiously checking each other out. All the clever things Murphy had practiced saying got scrambled in his head. Instead, he fumbled awkwardly while making inane comments as his son looked blankly back at him a quizzical look in his eyes. They made their way through their short time together before he returned the child safely to the front door of his new home.

Now, a year later, he was meeting to say goodbye. Forcing himself to do the deed he took the child's small hand in his. "Brian, I need to talk to you about something important." They were sitting on the top of a grassy mound watching three men in a kayak raise and dip their oars with delicate precision only slightly disturbing the river's tranquility. The child looked at him, smiling from ear to ear. "You're coming back to live with Mammy and me?" His lilting Cork voice hopefully asked. Merciful Jesus, Murphy wasn't prepared for that.

"No, Brian, I'm leaving for America. Tonight." The child looked back unblinking, then eerily smiled. Drawing his arms to his chest like a laid out dead person, he rolled spinning down the grassy bank. Murphy sat frozen as he observed what little that might have been left of his child's innocence being torn from him with each rotation of his young body.

His friends Nora and Bob lived in the Marina. The plan was for him to bring Brian back to their place after the chat. The boy pushed away Murphy's awkward attempt to take his hand and instead walked stiffly in front with head bent down. Murphy wanted to scream with the anger exploding inside, take the wounded child, wrap him protectively in his arms, tell him how much he loved him. But how could he justify such a bullshit claim when he was walking away and out of his life? So, he remained as silent as his child.

Nora had a kettle whistling when they knocked on the door. Awkwardly delaying the inevitable, Murphy stayed and drank cup after cup of unwanted tea. Brian gave him an occasional look, but his eyes turned cloudy and away from him on the rare occasion his father met his gaze. Mercifully, he eventually fell asleep on the couch. Now was the time for Murphy to leave. He held his child ever so gently in his arms one last time, kissed his left cheek softly terrified he'd wake him. Nora started crying at the door as she watched Murphy walk away down the road. He looked back briefly, then waved goodbye.

That same evening, he sat wordlessly with his mother in Limerick. Soon his brother would come to take him to the airport. Looking out, he was grateful to see a car pull up in the darkness outside. With difficulty, his mother stood up.

"I'll call you as soon as I get there and settled in."

"Please be careful, Lovey." She pushed a thick envelope into his coat pocket and was met with no resistance.

"I will, don't worry at all. They love the Irish over there. It'll all be grand, really." He smiled broadly, displaying more confidence than he felt, then picked up his light suitcase. He wondered should he kiss her goodbye, but that wasn't the way in Ireland. Any attempt at intimacy would have embarrassed both of them.

His brother came in the front door. Mother and her youngest child formally shook hands of farewell. She then dipped her fingers into the holy water font in the hallway that had a small statue of a sad looking Blessed Virgin Mary, dressed in blue and white. She then sprinkled holy water over him as she had done on any occasion since childhood when he was leaving home. Now he would be protected from all harm.

He waved to her from the gate. It pained him to see her hands over her mouth standing motionless under the hall doorway, watching her child embark on an uncertain future. He was broken inside, wanting to cry because he feared what was waiting nine thousand miles away, but also guilty for the pain he was causing her. But instead of breaking, he smiled brightly and, like a politician up for reelection, waved a hearty goodbye, then quickly disappeared into the oblivion his brother's car provided.

Murphy and his brother had a cup of tea at Shannon airport while waiting for his boarding call. Then they shook hands in farewell. "This will kill your mother." Were his brother's final words.

Soon the silver plane was shooting out over the Atlantic, distancing him with each second from his mother, from the small boy who was part of him, and from Ireland.

Chapter Two

EARLY CHILDHOOD

Ten black robed nuns with empty eye sockets, dark hoods concealing emaciated faces, laughed hysterically as they danced in a circle around the raging bonfire. Their gangly fingers pointed at Murphy as he screamed for mercy. The more frantically he begged, the angrier they became. "What are ye crying for, ye blabbering boy?" hissed the nuns as flames licked his feet. "This'll only last a short time, a bitin of pain, but yel have all eternity te burn in hell's everlastin fires!" More wood was thrown onto the mighty blaze that burned deeply into every bone in his body. His terrified screams could be heard in the next parish. Fighting against the ropes he was saved by waking.

He was five. Next morning would be his first day at school....with those scary nuns! Murphy was terrified at the thought of that first day away from his mother, and stories of the nun's barbarity haunted him. He'd been told them by his sister Grainne, always eager to discuss every lurid detail. One story she gleefully recalled was about two children, interestingly both boys, who had disappeared one night after being taken away for acts of subordination, whatever that meant. The nuns beat the children mercilessly; cut them into little pieces then sent the parts to the Pope in Rome. And in a few short hours Murphy would be at their mercy! Crawling deeper under his blankets he cringed with fear about the awaiting horrors.

Darkness would soon come. Scores of birds had already returned to the sanctuary of densely leaved trees.

The horn from the factory confirmed the end of the afternoon shift. Soon the sounds would reach him of workers panting and cursing as they cycled up the hill. Murphy looked out his bedroom window at the giant poplar trees that stood proudly along both sides of the avenue. They reminded him of old sailing ships with full sails swaying in the mounting evening breeze. Below that was the Dock Road. The factory his father ran stretched down to the towering Ranks flour mills. Because his father was so tall, the workers called him the Longfellah. Murphy was known as the Longfellah's son. Smoke from the factory chimneys rose, unobstructed, into the sky dark, cold and forbidding. Further over was the dock for ships and the mighty Shannon river that widened sharply near Foynes before eventually emptying itself into the Atlantic Ocean.

A fat moon sat above his house throwing blinding light at him. Resigned to his fate, he lay waiting for the earth to turn so morning would inevitably come. Birds in the trees had fallen asleep. Even the dogs were silent. Downstairs the grandfather clock chimed ten. He vaguely heard the workers moving up the hill.

Murphy thought back with sadness to the good old days when life had been simple. He prayed, "Lord Jesus Christ, save me from the nuns-and please don't have mother fall out of her bed again tonight."

Chapter Three

JAMSIE

Jamsie O'Malley disappeared one evening. He was never seen nor heard from again. There was lots of talk on the Avenue about what had happened. Murphy knew a lot, never told anybody, but he's telling you now.

Jamsie used to live with his mammy in a small cottage on the nun's land. T'was off the road that swung snake like down the Avenue from the house of Murphy's childhood. Weather permitting, Mrs. O'Malley used sit outside the cottage sleeping her afternoon away, deeply molded into a chair that constantly complained under her weight. Passing by the cottage he'd see her as she'd wake from lazy slumber, raise her plump right hand over beady eyes to search out Jamsie as he worked in the fields. She was a woman with eyebrows bushy like a beard, low in height, large in body, and a magnificent head of silver hair. She reminded Murphy of a fidgety polar bear with large glasses resting near the end of her nose twisting nervously in the unaccustomed sunlight.

Jamsie was often plastered, but always gentle when full with drink. Murphy would help him find his way home as he staggered, pushing his bicycle while laughing his head off when the contrary bike wouldn't go where he wanted; then he'd hand him over to his embarrassed mother. Although Murphy was only a child, Mrs. O'Malley always called him Sir or Young Mr. Murphy. "Thank you, Mr. Murphy, yer very good an kind," she'd say before fiercely slapping Jamsie's downward-bowed face, leading him inside the cottage and ordering him to his virgin bed.

Jamsie was the nun's handyman. Did everything for them. There were buildings to repair, cows to milk and, depending on the season, sheep to shear. He did all of that, and more besides. During summertime, he'd cut three acres of hay all by himself. Murphy used to intently watch him sharpening his crescent shaped scythe with a stone before disappearing into the fields. Sometimes Jamie allowed Murphy to silently follow behind. The sun would glint onto his razor-sharp blade, reflecting dancing layers of gold as he swished and swayed in effortless motion while all before him bowed to his will, dancing momentarily into the red fingered summer sky before falling obediently to ground. Sometimes he'd let Murphy try the scythe, then they'd both roar laughing when the boy would inevitably fall because it was at least twice his size and way too heavy for him to hold, let alone work.

One summer day he was following in Jamsie's wake. The scythe was raised over the man's shoulder and was about to strike when he froze. Peeking out from the strands of hay was a rabbit with twitching ears and little babies. Murphy saw Jamsie's eyes light up with joy as he shushed with his fingers then pointed down while the poor creators sat paralyzed with fear. Then he moved back from them and chuckled quietly as they watched the rabbits frantically hop away through swaying, golden layers of hay.

Jamsie also took care of the gardens. They were his pride and joy. One blossom time, Murphy's hand disappeared into his friend's and he listened carefully while he was told names of all the flowers. Jamsie knew those names even in Latin, yet he had almost no schooling. Other times he'd spot Murphy on the road and call him over. With his face burned deep bronze from the summer sun and rivers of sweat dripping down his body, he'd pick daffodils, tulips, daisies, and bluebells from the nun's fields. "Take these to yer mammy. She's a real lady."

But Murphy never told his mother the flowers were from Jamsie. Whenever he handed over Jamsie's gift, she'd kneel and drag Murphy into her bosom, hugging him, nearly choking him to death, while the flowers covered them with an explosion of color and scent. It felt so good to be in her arms, so warm so safe with his head nestling calmly on her shoulder. So much better than when she hit him. Anyway, he didn't want her cuddling Jamsie instead. Besides, sometimes she'd reward her child with a sparkling glass of Lucozade and Boland's richly chocolate biscuits. Other times she'd cry. Murphy used to get scared, then try and understand what he'd done to hurt her.

"It's all right, Lovey, you've done nothing wrong today."

The night Jamsie disappeared, Murphy sat motionless outside on the stairs squinting through the slightly open living room door. He intensely listened while his Dad told Mammy what had happened. He'd been passing by the cottage on his way home when he came on Jamsie being hauled away by four big policemen.

"Thought they were going to murder poor old Jamsie. Split his head open with their batons. Heard bones break." His father's hand now raised before enthusiastically banging down on the other, all the better to make his point. "Jamsie's eyes were wild. Thought for a moment he was crazy or wild drunk, maybe both," He paused, caught in remembering, shook his head, sighed then continued, "Jamsie's mother, God rest her soul, had been stone dead for maybe a week before the nuns came looking for Jamsie because he hadn't turned up for work. They found him with his lifeless mother clutched in his arms, crying, screaming mammy mammy wake up!" He wouldn't let go. The police had to beat him to drag him off her. The sergeant told me she stank something disgusting. When they got him outside Jamsie spotted me and shouted over, 'Mr. Ryan, please help me and Mammy, Sir!' His eyes wild with terror, arms outstretched Christ like. But what could I do?"

"But what DID you do?" His mother sharply asked in a clipped tone, head motionless, one hand pressed against her side, the other covering her left cheek.

"Went up to the Sergeant who recognized me. Told me the whole story. As he was telling me, Jamsie broke free and ran back towards the cottage. The guards tried to stop him but he fought madder than a drunken tinker on fair day. They clubbed him till his face was battered and covered in blood. That's when I heard his bones break. 'Staying with Mammy. I'm staying with Mammy!' he kept screaming till they beat him unconscious. A terrible sight, altogether shocking to see." His father shook his head sadly as he carefully remembered every detail for retelling in the pub later that night.

Outside on the stairs Murphy bit into the arm of his jammies and cried without sound, thinking about gentle, harmless Jamsie being hurt so badly. Why did the police have to hit him so much? He'd always been nice to all the young lads on the avenue. He'd only laugh when he caught us playing in the nun's fields and never once told on them. When the nuns found their secret tree house and ordered him to cut it down he uncomfortably said, "Lad, it close to broke my heart to be told to do this. T'was good for you lads to have a special place like that." Then he put his arms around the child and cried as Murphy comforted the big man until he was done. He wasn't seen for days after that 'because he took off on an almighty tear. Now it was Murphy's turn to silently cry an ocean of tears for Jamsie as he wondered where his friend now was.

He waited till after they'd said the evening rosary before asking his mother if he could talk with her. Hoping to help Jamsie, he bravely decided to confess about all those flowers coming to her from Jamsie and not him but, when the moment came, he paused, terrified she'd take the whips to him in punishment for all his badness. Instead he quietly asked her when would Jamsie be coming back. She thought momentarily before reaching down and taking him into her protective arms.

"Ah sure, Lovey, I was always very fond of Jamsie."

"Is he gone from us? Is he dead? Where's he tonight?"

"Ah, Lovey, don't you worry about him. He'll be taken care of."

Murphy was angry and wondered why grown-ups never answered questions when they didn't want to and, unlike children, always got away with it.

For a good while after that night he kept asking about Jamsie but never got an answer. Eventually his mammy became angry at him for continually pulling on her dress demanding a reply that would never come.

"For goodness sake, Child, he was only a laborer!" she snapped with crimson face.

Something inside the child crumbled like a flower that had been roughly trampled. So, he stopped asking.

They never again had sight, sound nor mention of that person.

Chapter Four

IT NEVER HAPPENED

The child knew it was all his fault when the bang and her cries woke him from sleep. In contrast, the sound from his father's room was deep snoring probably sourced from a fill of drink. Shivering, Murphy forced himself out of his bed's warmth and followed the weeping sounds, pushed the door open and turned on the light. It was worse than usual. Sparkling red blood crawled out of her head, then wandered across her face, before spilling into the white carpet. She cried without sound. Parts of her blue and white nightgown changed color as the blood on the carpet soaked into it. She looked tiny; lying rumpled on the floor, fetal, her knees against her chest, arms folded. She shuddered, her eyes flickered open and tried to look up but eyelids closed as blood blocked her sight. Her right arm lifted inches then heavily dropped. Jagged pieces of a broken glass fell from her bloodied hand.

The oak nightstand lay over her. An empty bottle of Gordon's gin was partially covered by an overturned ashtray. Smoked Rothmans, mixed with gray ash, lay scattered over the carpet. One still smoldered. Murphy squashed it. The room, as always, stank horridly of stale cigarettes and sadness. Opened bottles with pills scattered their contents on the bed and across the floor. A cuckoo suddenly jumped out of the clock on the wall, fluttered its molding red wings, chirped three times while joyfully announcing it was three o clock.

"Lovey, it's you, isn't it? Please help me. I'm sorry,

sooo sorry." Slurred and mumbled words wet by tears and a bloodied mouth. Her face was already black and purple from the fall. One eye was completely closed. She looked deformed, like she'd been thrown onto the road from a speeding car.

This time he felt no pity. Worse, his mother disgusted him. He hated the bitch, was sick of struggling to pick her up during the night and putting her back to bed. A raging, blind anger settled on him. Sometimes at Holy Communion, when he had on his tongue the Body and Blood of his Lord Jesus Christ, he felt a strange yet beautiful feeling, as if he were approaching the gates of Heaven to meet God. But what he now felt was as powerful, but pure evil. He wanted to finish the job she had started; shove loads of those pills down her throat then kick her pathetic broken body and keep kicking until she was lifeless, broken into silent pieces. But instead a coldness replaced his anger. He felt indifferent, walked out of the room leaving her alone, still crying his name.

Back in his bedroom, hiding under the bedcovers, he managed to temporarily ignore her pathetic baby crying. Everything went blank for a while. Had he viciously kicked his mother? He should have stayed with her. Pulling the bedclothes over his head he ran his hands over his ears so he wouldn't be able to hear her wailing any more. But it was futile. "Lovey, child please." Her pleading, mixed with choking sobs, traveled beseechingly along the corridor and into his head. There was no escape.

He banged on his father's bedroom door. No movement from inside. His father was snoring in deep sleep. The light from the landing captured his face. The dental plate he used for missing teeth sat on his bedside table in a chipped glass. His upper lip quivered as bubbles formed then quickly burst showing the pink gap of empty gum where teeth used to be. A fierce smell of whiskey and stale Guinness hit the child every time his father breathed out. With no more time to lose he shook him awake. His father's eyes slowly opened then shut as he struggled to understand what was happening.

"It's Mum, she's hurt again." His father's eyes opened wider then looked blankly at his son. Cursing quietly under his breath, he hesitated for a moment then struggled out of bed, put on his night robe, and walked slowly over to his wife's bedroom. The child hurriedly returned to the temporary sanctuary of his own room and locked the door. Lying in the darkness he heard sounds but was unable to grasp what was being said. After a while he heard the floorboards creak as his father went downstairs, made a phone call, and then went back into his mother's room. She was still crying, but less frantically. Then quiet.

The child wondered what was going to happen this time. Eventually he heard a motorcar traveling down the hill. The gears changed noisily before the car stopped outside his home. Pulling the curtains back he saw Dr. McMahon opening their gate. It needed oiling. He'd heard it said he was not a good doctor but had a "wonderful bedside manner" whatever that meant.

His father greeted the doctor and they shared a brief, mumbled chat before the man went in alone to his mother's bedroom. That must have been embarrassing, because father was in the Rotary club with Dr. McMahon and his mother was on the women's committee with Mrs. McMahon.

The child lay in bed wondering what was happening and hoping his mother would be all right. Now he deeply regretted he'd left her alone. There was a knock on his door and his father came in.

"Will Mum have to go to the hospital?" he whispered.

His father didn't answer, just looked away then down at the floor. "Don't think so. Dr. McMahon is with her now. She's going to be all right. May need a few stitches and go away for a few days' rest until she's better. Go back to sleep now." He paused as if about to say something else then gave the thumbs up sign and closed the door to darkness.

Dr. McMahon came out and another low, muffled conversation happened downstairs in the hallway. Then the doctor's car took off up the hill and his father retreated to his room. Everything became silent. Some hours later as dawn began to overcome the darkness, and birds outside began to chirp, the child finally fell into a deep sleep.

Next day he had lunch at school instead of coming home. After class ended, his father collected him and they went, as custom required, into South's bar. His father read the Irish Times and gave the child the comic strip section that had Dennis the Menace. He loved reading that and enjoyed a bag of Taytos and a Miwadi lemon drink as he silently read. His father had his usual large whiskey and glass of Guinness.

The child waited patiently for news about his mother. They were almost home when, "Your mother is fine. She's just gone away for a rest. She told me to tell you she'll cook you a lovely rhubarb tart when she comes back." He smiled when he said this but the child intuitively sensed his father was feeling as sad as he was.

Twenty-two days later, without warning, his mother returned home. He knew the precise number because, before going to bed each evening, he checked off the days on his bedroom calendar. He'd wondered had she gone forever. If so, it was his fault. He was sitting alone in his bedroom wondering about her when he heard the front gate squeak open. There she suddenly was walking ahead of a taxi man who staggered up the path under the weight of three heavy suitcases.

The child was elated but also conflicted because, although he badly needed his mother, he also feared her. And he was haunted with guilt over his sin of leaving her alone lying bleeding on the floor. Eagerly shouting, "MUM!" he waved down from his bedroom window.

Puzzled, she looked up, following the sound of the

voice. She shielded her eyes then her face opened brightly like a flower before the sun.

"Hello, Lovey." She waved back. She was wearing a light summer dress, white with black polka dots all over it. Her face had cleared up, bronzed looking like dark leather. No bruises anywhere. A picture of health. Maybe she had gone to their summer home and been nourished by the Atlantic breeze.

He raced downstairs taking the steps two at a time and arrived in the hallway just as the key fitted into the door lock. "Mum, you're home. I'm sorry for everything."

She wrapped him in her arms, nearly squeezing him to death. He returned her affection with equal gusto. Looking closely, he noticed that despite the improvements, her eyes had retained their battered look. She put her fingers to his lips. Drawing back, he thought for a moment she was going to cry, but instead, thank God, she took his small hand in hers and said, "Let's go into the kitchen. I'll bake you a special pie."

Before he dozed off that night, his stomach full with rhubarb pie and lashings of fresh cream mixed with sugar, his mother came in to check on him. He pretended to be asleep but she knew he wasn't. Her hand was damp as she stroked his forehead before kissing it with lips that barely touched. She stood for a minute looking quietly down at him. He sensed she wanted to say something important. but she said nothing, only sighed before leaving. He sneaked his eyes open just a little, and saw her looking back at him in the half-light thrown from the landing.

"Good night, love you," she whispered in a solemn, tender voice, so low he never heard her.

Chapter Five

THE FARM

Most summers in Murphy's childhood he was sent to stay for a few weeks with his relations on the farm in county Kildare. "We Irish are basically an agrarian people. It's important to get yer hands dirty, to get close to the land!" his father used enthusiastically announce every year while impeccably dressed in his three-piece suit, sparkling polished shoes, nails glistening from manicure, his unlined face beaming with unbridled enthusiasm, hands clasped tightly, before putting his young child on the Dublin train then hastily departing. The fact that he had rarely if ever set foot on any farm land, and only then for a few hours, never diminished his enthusiasm for "the land." He was convinced his excellent stewardship of the back garden at home, which yielded an abundance of healthy vegetables, more than qualified him as a bone fide farmer only temporarily absent from his imaginary acreage.

Murphy loved those visits, they would take a lifelong place of appreciation in his memory. But his older sister Grainne detested most rural aspects and refused to return after only one short summer visit to the farm. What was an adventure to his young mind was grossly uncivilized for a young lady of her stature. She was horrified by the absence of indoor toilets and rarely missed the opportunity to complain about the undignified and primitive act of having to go into the fields to do her business. "And grass, GRASS we had to use to try and clean ourselves!" she'd wail, her voice a demented banshee, her face a bucket of mortal sins twisted in agony, crumpled like a burned rasher for anyone willing to listen and also to those who were not.

His silent, gentle brother Liam, eldest of them, visited one year and never complained. Instead he'd sit, comfortable in his isolation, while lost in the book his bespectacled face was usually buried into. He was beyond shy and would usually blush when spoken to. His was unquestioned acceptance of any condition that presented itself. Later, he would be sent away to boarding school with the Cistercian Brothers in Roscrea to "broaden his social skills." Whatever that meant Murphy could not determine.

An upside to the visits for him was he only got the occasional beating from Aunt Pearl, although he was terrified of her as he was of most adult women. Besides, it was peaceful being away from the violence and noise at home and he loved the canal which meandered down from Dublin through the bog land, with locks every few miles. Powerful horses with ropes attached to barges, silently moved along beside the canal that flowed behind the farmhouse. Often Murphy would wait patiently for them to come, growing ever so slowly from specs in the distance, until voices of the men began to carry over the water. Then, after a lifetime of waiting, they'd finally come into view, huge, God like creatures, made gigantic by the sun at their backs. The water reflected sparkling light up and onto them causing them to disappear, then reappear, giants made gloriously bright, magnified by the summer evening, and welcomed by a symphony of birds. Murphy would see all this as well as pond ducks scattering into careful seclusion, and the canal's smooth surface rippling from an approaching barge.

Sometimes they'd let him on until the next lock and tell him of their adventures. He'd then slowly walk back along the bank in the encroaching darkness, chewing on every word they'd told him about the world beyond, while unconsciously observing the sights and sounds of nature preparing for sleep.

The canal was always full with many types of lively fish. All they had to do was throw in a line and there'd immediately be something jigging on it that Aunt Pearl would cook.

They'd swim there on the odd occasion when they had time. Murphy used to love floating dreamingly, looking up into the summer sun comfortably at peace. Sometimes clouds floated overhead, white elephants and bears or hands with fingers silently calling him to play.

Aunt Pearl was his father's only sister. Another had fallen into a boiling vat at age six then died after her screams had softened to a whimper. Aunt Pearl had somehow met and married Uncle Frank, moving from working class Dublin to begin life on a few, poor, farming acres on the Bog of Allen. As the name implied it was primarily bog land but, through back breaking work over many years, they had survived and even clawed their way to add more acreage.

Eventually, despite the harshness of the land, they had become completely self-sufficient, with sheep, cattle, and fields of barley and hay depending on the season. All this provided a meager but sufficient income. Aunt Pearl raised hens that gave fresh eggs daily, chickens she would kill as needed, fresh milk from the cows that went into the making of beautiful butter, and fresh cream that fell onto steaming rhubarb pies, the wonder of which Murphy never experienced before then or indeed later in his life. In a sty, there was also a sow that produced piglets each year which were either eaten at home or sold at market.

All the work was done manually. It was a time long before tractors. Uncle Frank's only help being Harry, his horse used for tilling the fields. Murphy used to watch him walk in a perfect line behind Harry talking in special words, sometimes in tender voice, other times in harsh, urging him on line after line until either darkness or another task demanded Uncle Frank's attention.

His uncle was a gentle giant of a man. Despite the daunting tasks that constantly faced him, it always seemed to Murphy that he was at peace or about to break out into boisterous laughter. But he was not smiling when Harry got sick from age and he had to put a bullet in his head. Since no words were spoken about it, Murphy wondered if firing the shotgun had broken his uncle's heart, or at least hurt him for a while. But it was impossible to know. Just as in his home certain matters were never discussed.

Everyone had to work at harvest time. Tradition required neighbors from all surrounding farms to come over to help save the hay and other crops. Usually it took up to a week, then everyone would move onto the next small farm, then the one after that, until all had been cared for.

Murphy was too young to do hard work but they kept him busy one way and another. No hands were left idle. Despite his minimal workload, he was always relieved when we saw, shrouded in early afternoon heat, shimmering figures laden with heavy luncheon baskets floating unevenly towards them. Women's voices mixed with young girl's squeals, now conflicted with groans from the older men in the fields around him who stretched their backs and spat on their hands, grateful of the chance to briefly rest. Out would come the Woodbines and they'd light up. Usually only the men and boys worked while the women of each farm were responsible for feeding the small army that annually descended into their world. Great rivalry existed to provide the best food but Murphy always thought Aunt Pearl's won easily.

Scalding hot tea flowed from thick cisterns into enamel mugs. Sugar and milk mixed to make a decent brew. Chunks of chicken bulged between slices of homemade, brown, soda bread only to quickly disappear down throats that then demanded more. Apple and rhubarb pies overflowed with layers of freshly made cream, scones barely out of the oven melted Aunt Pearl's butter, then were topped off with jam made from the raspberry bushes that prospered in her garden.

Silence, mixed with a sense of calm, settled on the fields during eating time. The only sounds were of distant cows, faraway bleating sheep, and the lazy twitter of birds among the tree branches under which the community sought shade. Any attempt at horseplay between the older boys and girls was quickly put down. This was a serious time and not an occasion for sin.

But what a transformation when the fields had been saved, the barn filled, and another harvest completed! After they had gone to work on the surrounding farms and returned their help, a party was held to celebrate. The women brought all kinds of mouth-watering dishes so the table seemed to sink with the weight of them. Drink flowed, and men known for their musical ability were called on to play. Fiddles, mandolins, banjos, and bowrans filled the night with lively tunes while young men and women danced wildly under the watchful eyes of mothers and fathers anxious for a good match. Many of those nights, Murphy would fight hard to stay awake before finally succumbing to the limitations of his years and reluctantly trundle off to bed.

One special Wednesday, Murphy awoke, excited, knowing he was going to accompany his uncle and cousins to the fair at Newbridge. For him it would be an exhilarating experience. He'd been looking forward to it for weeks and had barely slept a wink. None of his friends in the city could tell a cow from a bull any more than he could before he began to come to the farm, and any chance to learn more was an adventure for him.

Soon he was shivering from morning chill and excitement as he followed, with his cousins, behind Uncle Frank through the bustling crowd, skipping three steps to each one of his leisurely gait. All the while he looked about him, soaking in the atmosphere and stew of rich, wonderful smells of animals and leather, sweat and hay, pipe tobacco and porter. Noise was everywhere: the voices of men arguing about prices, calculated insults exchanged and pretended offense taken, the nervous, high-pitched neighing of horses and the desperate bawling of barely weaned calves crying for their mothers, sheep bleating and older cows, no longer with milk, bawled, knowingly destined for the slaughterhouse.

Thatchers with magical hands strolled amongst the crowd calling for roofs to mend with their straw. Fiddle and banjo players made music at every corner, one pretending not to notice the other while desperately trying to outdo his rival; and the pubs overflowed with drink and farmers whose deals were done. Tinkers sold pots, pans, and the occasional horse; the tinker men striding with unusual dignity alongside their flaming red-haired women whose mysterious wild beauty fascinated Murphy.

When asked, Uncle Frank told him they could well be descended from the old Chieftain families.

"What happened to them?"

"After the English came and threw the Catholics off their lands they brought in the planters, Protestants from Scotland, so people who were farmers took to the roads. Worked with tin making pots, pans and the like so were called Tinkers. Never found their way back to the land." At this he paused and a dreamy look of sadness settled momentarily on him. "Without the land, you're nothing," he said, almost to himself. It was the closest to being philosophical he ever became while in Murphy's presence.

He knew Uncle Frank had come to buy some heifers but regardless of whether he was buying or selling, his uncle adopted a casual air so it was impossible for Murphy to tell if he was truly interested in any offer being made. He watched with wonder Uncle's seeming indifference as sellers responded to his queries about their beasts, and it took him some time to realize that everybody, either buying or selling, behaved in a similar manner. He was unknowingly witnessing a centuries old tradition which, although this was serious business, contained elements of theater, gamesmanship, cunning and relationship-building all rolled into the occasion.

It was said that Uncle Frank had a good eye for a decent animal and finally he spotted three he liked. He whispered his interest to Murphy and his cousins who watched carefully as the big man sauntered nonchalantly past a grinning, toothless man with twine holding his tattered coat in place and a thick ash plant stick in his left hand.

"Good day to ye, Frank. How's Pearl? My Ghod, dose sons o' yours are growin' into mighty men, mighty men altageder. An' who's the little fella?" he asked with a smile that could light the world if needed. Murphy extended his hand and was properly introduced.

"Are ye buyin' or sellin' teday, Frank?" knowing full well why Uncle was there.

Usually a man of utmost politeness and gentility, Uncle Frank surprised Murphy by responding, "Well Thomas, I was thinkin' of maybe buyin' but don't see anythin' worth the time."

Thomas became transformed, his body racked in pain. His mouth opened in astonishment, pencil sized lips flapped to display toothless gums then shut again. The sunshine look disappeared to be replaced by a look of righteous indignation. "My God man don't ye see de mighty offering I hav here behind me? They're more precious te me dan me own children an' a sight more useful. It breaks my heart but if ye make a decent offer I might, just might, mind ye, tink about lettin em go."

Uncle Frank sighed and took a brief glance at the animals. "Look a bit weak. Did they not winter well?"

Thomas cowered, reacting as if Uncle Frank had beaten him savagely over the head. "Man dear, day'll fetch de best price teday!"

Murphy believed he was about to launch into an extensive explanation of his cattle's superb pedigree dating back to before the Druids when Uncle Frank politely bade him goodbye for now, and offered to buy him a drink later. The look of devastation on Thomas›s face made Murphy feel really sad for him so, as they were walking away, he shouted back at him, «Uncle Frank really likes your cows. He wants to buy them.»

Although heated discussions and bargaining had been going on all around us now, suddenly, there was dead quiet.

Thomas' face broke into another great smile and he beamed at Murphy. "So, he does, does he? Well yer uncle always was a good man te judge a dacent animal. Isn't dat right, Frank?"

With that the crowd around burst into a storm of laughter. Uncle Frank didn't join them as he dragged Murphy away. He led him around a corner, bent down from the clouds, his hand weighing on Murphy's head, and said in a barely audible but steel-like voice, "When I'm after an animal you will NEVER talk or say ONE word."

Murphy's cousins sniggered at him behind their dad then turned away in disgust when the city boy suddenly burst into tears. All Murphy knew was that he'd done something wrong to anger this special man. Horrified, he didn't dare speak a word for the rest of that day. Instead he quietly observed a centuries old tradition and wondered at its seemingly endless complex contradictions.

His Uncle Frank eventually bought the three calves. But the process took an unbelievably long time with endless discussions, walking away, shaking of heads in disbelief, and multicolored disparaging remarks about the quality of the beasts on offer. When Uncle Frank first asked the price of the three calves he almost collapsed with laughter at the amount mentioned. Waving his arm in farewell he strode off in absolute disgust. It was then that a little man mysteriously appeared on the scene. Murphy thought it a coincidence, but learned later that he had been carefully watching for the right time to approach. It was his job to bring the parties together.

"Ah sure, Frankie, make the man a sound offer." He tugged on Uncle Frank's arm as he strode away. Murphy searched uncle's face for any sign of interest but saw only complete indifference.

"Patrick, I'm looking maybe for a few calves that'll make me a dacent few pound next yare. I'm not here to lose the farm."

"I KNOW that Frank, sure we all have ta live but don't insult the poor fellow, at least offer him something."

That seemed to have an impact on Uncle Frank and, reverting to the polite man he was, and not wanting to insult a fellow farmer, he relented. "All rite, tell him I'll give him fifty pound fer the lot."

"Jazas Frank I couldn't go back ta him wit dat! Let me tell him eighty, no let's say seventy."

"Tell him sixty an dat's more dan there's worth. Times are bad, God knows, and dats a lot more dan he'll get."

Now it was the middleman's turn to stride across the stage.

The next hour was spent with the little man moving back and forth between the parties while Murphy and his cousins stood watching, learning the ancient skills they would need when their time came.

Finally, after leading the calves away then being called back, after being given a final offer of seventy pounds, and insisting he couldn't budge for anything less than ninety, the calves were sold for eighty, a price both men apparently knew all the time they would agree upon. The middleman brought Uncle Frank and the other man together and took their right arms in his little hands. "So we hav a dael, an agreement is in place, right!" he shouted.

The two men towered over him like embattled prizefighters, eyes locked one on the other, sadness and desperation pouring from every fiber because of the terrible price being paid and the pitiful one being received. Murphy couldn't believe what was happening. Both men's heads nodded almost imperceptibly. The middleman raised their arms over his head, swung them down and all three spat on their respective palms before bringing them together with a resounding crash. Smiles broke out, bank notes exchanged hands, Uncle Frank and the seller suddenly seemed like long lost best friends having suddenly found each other. Then off with all of them to the pub to toast the deal. Uncle Frank wasn't much of a drinking man but courtesy demanded he share a pint or three.

Murphy noticed the man gave Uncle Frank crumpled notes and asked why. "T'is good luck money for the sale. I'd give it te him if sellin mine."

The bar was noisy, smoky, bouncing with music, triumphant shout when hitting 45 in a card game, uneven laughter, usually reserved but now boisterous men caught up in the moment. Sons carefully observed, learning a tradition they, and their sons, would honor when their time came.

Chapter Six

MACBETH

Life on the farm was always hard. Every day was a series of ongoing, backbreaking chores, while the animals required constant attention. There was little room for frivolity and each waking moment was limited to within the property's borders. Pleasures from the world beyond the farm had little place in the daily struggle for survival. But one summer an incident occurred which had a profound lifelong effect on Murphy. It happened one night in a small, overfilled, boisterous village hall.

A new curate had arrived the year before. Murphy had briefly met him after Mass one Sunday. He was from a small farm in county Cork so he understood his parishioners and knew on a firsthand basis the hardships of their lives, their foibles, fears, and joys. Murphy had instantly been drawn to his boyish laughter and joy of life. Being only six, he appreciated the way Fr. Joyce talked to him as a real person and not a stupid child in the way of most adults. Later that morning he overheard Aunt Pearl suggest that the new curate had better be careful with all his modern ideas. "Won't sit well with Fr. Reilly," she suggested, lips tightly drawn while vigorously shaking her head as she set the lunch plates.

Uncle Frank muttered, "Aye, aye," while buried deep in the sports section of the Sunday Independent.

"He's talkin' about arrangin' dances for the young people and doin' plays."

That caught Uncle Frank's attention. "All the music better be Irish and the plays too if he ever wants to get it off the ground," he laughed amused by the situation.

It was well known that the parish priest detested any culture that wasn't Irish. He despised the barbarian English for what they had done to his sacred country and wanted nothing to do with them. His favorite topic was ranting against them. "What's the point of us defeating the Sasanagh and banishing them forever from most of our island?" Here he'd sigh and lament the occupied northern counties, "As if our own culture wasn't good enough for us? They tried to destroy us any way they could. They starved us, murdered us, took away our language, our way of life, but they failed to exterminate us. Why, we had laws, the Brehon Laws, a thousand years before the Englishman was even walking upright. And Stonehenge! Newgrange, only a stone's throw from our own parish, predates that English place by over a thousand years! Stonehenge is a brand-new building compared to it. English culture my arse!" And with that he'd storm off, overflowing with righteous indignation and his face a throbbing red with veins ready to explode.

Apparently, Fr. Joyce, despite the danger of it leading to an occasion of sin for the parish youth, had been granted permission to introduce Irish dancing. The parish even put on a play called "Playboy of the Western World". Since an Irish playwright wrote it the Monseigneur considered it safe and decent. All the farming community had come together and got caught up in the excitement of temporarily transforming themselves from the drabness and severity of their everyday existence.

The following year Fr. Joyce somehow received permission to put on an English play! Murphy wondered how he had done that. Perhaps Fr. Reilly secretly hoped it would be a disaster. Although he appreciated the easing of his workload, maybe he didn't like his new curate's enormous energy, was suspicious of his newfangled ideas, and somewhat jealous of his growing popularity with the people. Murphy overheard Aunt Pearl say that the word on the wind was that Fr. Reilly had become worn down from his years of service and simply wanted some quiet time before being put out to pasture and leaving his flock to another man, provided his replacement was sound.

Much to the consternation of Uncle Frank and the cousins, his Aunt Pearl auditioned for, and got a part in the play. They began rehearsing a few days after Murphy arrived for his summer trip. He couldn't remember Aunt Pearl even reading a book but this time it seemed she had her nose constantly stuck in a thick mass of pages reading, nodding her head, squinting her eyes, and repeating unrecognizable words in low tones none of the lads could properly hear. They laughed a lot nervously behind her back thinking she'd gone a little daft.

For six weeks Aunt Pearl had regularly disappeared after dinner and headed out on her bicycle to peddle furiously down past the canal, out the laneway and up the hill to the village hall where rehearsals were taking place. As opening night grew closer her nightly departures increased. Uncle Frank and the lads weren't thrilled about this, but knew better than to complain. Although Murphy loved his Aunt Pearl she also terrified him with her stern look and he thought the lads wise not to protest. Besides, she always provided an excellent dinner prior to her departure.

He believed Aunt Pearl had really gone bonkers in the week before the opening. She snapped at everybody more than usual, wandered about the house muttering lines to herself, and cursed her stupidity for getting caught up in the curate's damned play.

The night of the dress rehearsal she completely lost it after coming home and started shouting at poor Uncle Frank as if it were all his fault. This giant of a man, who could break any man's neck at will, looked unspeaking across the room at his city wife's shoes as she ranted and raved. ''Tis a disaster.

People don't have a clue of their lines. Mother of God we'll be a laughing stock in every parish. No! Throughout the entire county!" With that she charged past, slammed the door of her bedroom, and wouldn't come out. Murphy was sure he heard her crying. Uncle Frank, the lads, and Murphy sat around the sweet-smelling turf fire silently looking into the embers and totally at a loss. None recognized the mad woman she'd become. What was her problem? Damn that Fr. Joyce! Why couldn't he have left well enough alone?

Before she left the next night, a Friday it was, Aunt Pearl ordered the lads to scrub themselves before putting on their Sunday best. There were no toilets or hot water in the cottage so they had to stand in line while Aunt boiled water then scrubbed them down. Murphy was embarrassed being naked in front of her but she just laughed and told him she'd known him since he was a baby so to stop being stupid. Despite that reassurance, Murphy quickly used a towel to cover his embarrassment.

The boys were ordered under pain of immediate death to behave themselves and not disgrace her before everybody. Then off she went on her bicycle while the boys waited for Uncle Frank to finish getting ready. He eventually rambled into the kitchen, cursing his failure to make the top button of his shirt meet the buttonhole. But finally, all were dressed in their very best and ready for the road.

When they arrived at the village hall they were greeted at the door by a neighbor from a few fields over who gave them a program typed unevenly in black and white. As they took their seats Murphy scanned the pages and there was Aunt Pearl's name! He recognized most of the other people mentioned and trembled with anticipation of the unknown that was about to unfold. The hall quickly filled with what seemed like overly enthusiastic conversations. He wondered did anybody have a clue what the play was about and had the families of the other actors experienced the same contrariness inside their homes as they had. All the men and boys were dressed in suits and looked as uncomfortable as Murphy felt, while the women and girls were dressed up in their best finery. It was like attending Sunday mass.

The parish priest sat in the middle of the front row reading the program notes with an intense look on his face. Beside him in the blocked off, reserved seats sat the local doctor and to his right the bank manager from the nearest town. The village was too insignificant to warrant a branch office. Next to the banker was Bertie "The Nose" Kearns, the solicitor who did most of the farm sales and estate law in the area. Between them, they knew all the dirty secrets and dealings of everyone in the hall. Finally, the lights were dimmed, then turned off. Boisterous laughter and conflicting chatter died away to be replaced by a potent air of nervous expectancy. Safe now in darkness, most of the men quickly unbuttoned the necks of their unfamiliar shirts.

Thunder rumbled and lightening flashed.

Murphy wriggled eagerly in his sixth-row seat squished between his cousins. Uncle Frank sat behind. At first Murphy was acutely aware of his inhibiting presence, but he was soon forgotten as the curtains were slowly drawn back and the magic began.

"When shall we three meet again, in thunder, lightning or in rain?"

Silence settled on the hall where all inside were instantly transported from their grimy, flat bog land into a swirling, mysterious world of babbling witches. Murphy's mouth hung open as he gazed intently at the developing scene.

Vaguely he recognized two of the witches stirring a large pot and craned forward, fascinated, until those last rasping words:

"Fair is foul and foul is fair,
Hover through the fog and filthy air."

The scene quickly changed to men talking, obviously tired toward the end of a journey and, although he was unable to understand a lot of the words, the sense of excitement and power of the moment were inescapable to even his most innocent ear. Then the witches reappeared, scarier than ever, cackling about ships and killing pigs, and all kinds of weird things until they met and began to talk to the men who seemed happy to hear whatever it was the witches told them was going to happen.

Murphy began to worry about his aunt. Where was she? He tried to whisper to his cousin but a strong poke in the back from Uncle Frank stopped that. Aunt must have a very small part to not have appeared yet. But suddenly there she was, in a dark room all by herself reading a letter. She read it aloud and Murphy almost shouted out, "It's Aunt Pearl!" But it no longer was Aunt Pearl. That hard-working woman, who toiled uncomplainingly from dawn 'til dusk, had become transformed into a magical, elegant proud presence. She strode across the stage, speaking in a voice full of fire, "Glamis thou art, and Cawdor, and shalt be what thou art promised." Soon she was majestically commanding her husband, Macbeth, and Murphy saw by her regal carriage that she was a true lady. Her fine purple gown contrasted with the dark hair which cascaded down to her waist, making her a woman of immense power and beauty. He sat transfixed as the play progressed, enveloped in the palpable sense of awe, which had settled over the hall.

These were men and women with whom he had worked in the fields and, although they loved to talk and were unknowingly philosophical, they seldom had time to read books. Yet here they sat enthralled by the drama displayed before them. Midway through the performance he stole a quick look back at Uncle Frank and could swear he saw him quickly wipe away a tear.

The fact that Murphy didn't understand a lot of what

was being said didn't matter, the words sounded so grand and powerful. He shared Macbeth's horror when he came back after murdering the king. Murphy understood how guilty he felt when he kept trying to wash the imaginary blood off his hands. Lady Macbeth tried to cheer him up but Murphy could see that even though he got to be king he was miserable, and it was awful when he ended up killing his best friend who then came back as a ghost.

To be sure, everything went wrong for the poor man, and then Lady Macbeth, who had always been so strong, began walking about in her sleep trying to wipe imaginary blood off her hands, and letting out secrets about the murder. Murphy knew she was wicked yet tasted salt in his throat when she said in such a small, sad voice, "Here's the smell of blood still; all the perfumes of Araby will not sweeten this little hand - oh, oh, oh."

After that, an army disguised as a forest attacked the castle and there was a big fight. It was very exciting and the audience cheered whenever someone killed someone else. They knew Macbeth was dead when his lopped off head was carried in by a lad called Macduff. At first Murphy thought it was real but of course it was only something the priest had made from some old sacking and a helmet. To be sure it looked enough; in fact, everything did for a while there. He even forgot that Lady Macbeth was his aunt.

After a final flourish of trumpets there were a few moments of silence, then the hall went mad with cheering, whistling and foot stomping. They were still clapping when, after five curtain calls, the actors decided they'd had enough and headed backstage.

When Aunt Pearl came home later that night he saw her with different eyes. She had cycled away from the cottage that evening as his aunt, a simple woman he mistakenly thought he'd known well all his young life. But a few hours later, she returned as a woman of mystery, a person of amazing depth, talent - and beauty. She had become forever transformed in his mind. He understood that he would never look at her in the same way again.

Chapter Seven

CHRISTMAS IN DUBLIN

"We'll stay up there for a few days then come back on the twenty-third," his father told them. It was the week before Christmas and they were going up to Dublin, far across the entire country, almost one hundred and twenty miles away, the big city, there to stay with his beloved Granny. So exciting! They'd climb up to the top of Nelson's Pillar, get fish and chips at one of the Italian chippers on O'Connell Street, then go shopping on bustling Moore Street. Adding to his excitement his mother's brother, Uncle Paddy, would take them out to a pantomime at the Gaiety Theater where Jimmy O'Dea, Maureen Potter, and Des Keogh were starring in Mother Goose.

"Rockin' around the Christmas tree at the Christmas party hop," Brenda Lee enthusiastically belted out from the crystal radio set as he patiently waited in the living room with his parents, gentle brother Liam, and his sister Grainne. Since Artic below zero temperatures had made the roads unpassable, Joe Broderick from his father's factory would bring them to the train station.

Thinking about sins that might endanger getting the presents he had asked Santa for, with both arms resting on knees, lost in his own world, Murphy solemnly reflected on the year just passed. Yes, he had unsuccessfully tried on two occasions to murder his big sister Grainne, an offense from which any jury would not only have acquitted him but would have enthusiastically applauded him for at least trying. And hadn't he confessed everything to the priest in confession so if God forgave him surely Santa also would? Exhaling deeply, he began to feel cautiously optimistic.

Nervously anticipating the unknown, he hadn't slept much the night before. Compared to Limerick town, Dublin, the capital city, was gigantic. He was terrified, but didn't dare tell anyone, that if he got lost in the swaying crowds he'd never again see his family. And making the experience stranger was he often couldn't understand what Dublin people were saying because of the strange way they talked, so if he did get lost, they mightn't be able to understand him or he them.

Finally, Joe Broderick rang the doorbell. The previous night he'd overheard his father say that he needed to put some distance between Joe Broderick and himself; he was "becoming far too familiar." His father had helped Joe Broderick a lot, had even paid him all his wages when a truck he had been working on in the factory fell on his leg and smashed it. Murphy didn't know what "too familiar" meant and when he asked the meaning was abruptly told "not to be spying on adult conversations."

Joe carried their suitcases out to the car, put them in the boot, and off they went. Murphy waved to some of his friends on the Avenue who had gathered to see him off on his adventure. "See you next week," he shouted hoping he would.

Within five minutes they arrived at Colbert station. While Joe got a trolley, they brought the suitcases to the train's first class section. His father ushered them into the railway bar for a drink. It was especially busy at that time of year and loud with chatter and laughter. A big Christmas tree covered in tinsel, bulbs and sparkling lights twinkled in the corner. Under the tree, Murphy counted numerous gift packages wrapped in red paper and brown twine.

As usual the Dublin train was behind schedule. If it arrived twenty minutes' late it was considered a half hour early. The children went back out onto the platform with their mother while his father and Joe Broderick remained in the bar for a Christmas drink or three. Under their mother's watchful eye, the children chased each other and played hide and seek. When the train finally puffed into the station Murphy was sent to get his father. The bar sounding loud with boisterous, seasonal bonhomie, was cloudy from men smoking either cigarettes or pipes. He had to excuse himself several times as he made his way through towards his father.

"Oh, you're right there, Sir." Joe was saying. More men pushed their way into the bar as they left. His father thanked Joe for driving them. "Happy Christmas Joe," while shaking his hand. Murphy noticed the corner of a ten-punt note sticking out of Joe's fist. "Bye now, Joe, we'll see you when we get back." So much for the planned distancing of Joe, the boy briefly thought.

"Thanks very much Sir." Joe bowed his head while doffing his ragged cap, then away with him out of the station with a smile on his face.

There weren't many people going to Dublin, most were returning from working in the big city. "We'll have the train to ourselves," said his father who was in an especially vibrant mood after the drink. Parents and girlfriends, all who had been waiting impatiently, now got their reward as, one by one, beaming and expectant faces came off the train, scanned the crowd wondering, and were recognized with shouts of happy welcome. "There he is, yoo-hoo, Jerry, over here," and "Tommy, ya blind bastard, have ye forgotten us already?"

Shouts of delight rang out. "I saw Mommy kissing Santa Clause," blared from the loud speaker. Everybody smiled. It was a happy time.

"Last call for Dublin and Cork. Change at Limerick Junction for both Dublin and Cork. All aboard, all aboard," shouted the conductor. His whistle blew and away they finally went on their adventure.

The train coughed reluctantly out of the station. It was six o'clock, dark, and a light mist followed as they chugged along. On their right, owned by the Crescent Jesuit School, was the clubhouse and pitch where Murphy played rugby and was team captain. His brother never played rugby. He was too fragile but Murphy wasn't. He was strong, could change the outcome of a game with one startling move, was fearless, and would tackle anybody regardless of size.

Further out were the corporation houses where lots of his father's workers lived. Those houses looked sad, bleak, and boringly similar. Enormous numbers of baby's nappies and clothes were getting wet trying to dry themselves hanging on the garden clotheslines. Then suddenly, there was only darkness and no lights from the city to show the outside world. Liam and Grainne played cards but Murphy dozed off soothed by the clickety-clack music of the rails.

Half an hour later the train slowed and pulled into Limerick Junction where they had another drink before catching the connecting train to Dublin.

Murphy fell asleep for a minute. Next thing he knew Grainne was kicking him awake. He howled but she told him not to be such a crybaby.

"You're to wake up. We're almost in Dublin station. Dad, he's not waking up," she whined as his father arrived back from the bar, coming in with a glowing look.

Rubbing his eyes, he looked out the window. Dublin was different. It took forever to get from the outskirts to the station. Orange lights brightened the railroad tracks and the houses and flats that ran beside them for miles and miles, only ending when they arrived at Houston. More orange lights lit up the streets and roads. Nothing like that in Limerick. He searched out his mother and grabbed her hand tightly. Didn't want to get lost.

His father's only bachelor brother, Uncle Joe, was

waiting for them on the platform. He lived with Granny. Once he'd heard his Granny say to father, "If he gets married never will there be a need to rush for the mid-wife." Uncle Joe used to go door to door selling vacuum cleaners, but Murphy couldn't see him ever selling anything. Somehow, though, he'd made a lot of money and eventually owned a big petrol station.

His face was tightly screwed up into one nasty frown. He was always grumpy and clearly unhappy to see the children. A mean person, not at all like his father's other six brothers who were mighty craic. He also disliked animals. One time, when visiting Granny, Murphy had seen Uncle Joe savagely kick and kill a kitten that had got in his way.

He pretended to smile but it had the warmth of an iceberg. Murphy knew he didn't want them there interfering with his privacy. He despised children even more than defenseless animals. "We haven't a snowball's chance in hell of getting the Christmas shilling off him," Grainne complained as they trotted after his impatient stride to the car. There wasn't much room so they squeezed on top of one other down by the Grand Canal for the twenty-minute journey to his grandmother's house.

Murphy was nervous, excited, tired and feeling car sick. "Think I'm going to vomit," this to his mother. Uncle Joe cursed, not bothering to hide his displeasure, then opened the window to let a blast of freezing air blow in. Although Murphy welcomed it everybody else roared "Close please!" They drove on a busy O'Connell Street teeming with Christmas shoppers and bright holiday decorations, then up the hill before arriving at De Coursey Square in Glasnevin. The houses were old but sturdy two-storied red brick, going around in a square with a garden patch running along the middle where all the neighbors planted vegetables they shared.

His beloved grandmother was waiting at the front

door. They competitively ran to be the first to wrap themselves around her tidy frame. They loved her very much. She never got angry with them and her food was plentiful and delicious. Besides, she always gave them money when they left. After disengaging herself from the children she hugged her dutiful, eldest son and, having forgotten to put in her false teeth, gave him toothless kisses.

His grandfather had died a few years before. Murphy's only memory was walking along the bank of the Royal canal on a burning hot summer day, his hand lost in the big carpenter's, a hand that felt like a boulder. He smelled of stale tobacco and wore a thick suit and tweed cap that must surely have been uncomfortably warm.

There was rarely silence when they visited his grandmother's house. That day was no exception. No sooner were they in the door than they were stumbling to avoid crawling babies and bumping into nephews and nieces from several counties. Sounds of all sorts battled for prominence: laughter, shouting, arguments, children squealing, all engulfed them as they stumbled along the hall corridor.

Christmas was a time when the tribe gathered from far and wide. But this Christmas was extra special as his grandmother was celebrating her seventy fifth birthday, so no one dared be absent. His father, eight brothers, with wives and children in tow, descended on the house that December to eat and drink a delighted grandmother out of house and home. Traditionally the men and boys headed out to the pub immediately after dinner while the women and girls remained at home cleaning up and complaining about the men.

Although the house was of decent size, sleeping accommodation was a major challenge. The men were segregated from the women with four or five packed into each bed, alternating head to toe. Murphy laughed quietly as he listened to the varied pitches of snoring coming from the older men in the room.

That small army of relatives somehow found a place to lie down and sleep in that magical Christmas house. During the first night Murphy woke to find that a male relative was sleeping beside him in the overcrowded bed and was touching Murphy's private parts. Frightened and clueless about what to do, he simply froze while also feeling ashamed at his response. Moments later he pushed the hand away, escaped out of the bed and tried unsuccessfully to sleep on the cold floor for the remainder of the night.

Early morning light crept into the room, the milkman with horse and cart clicked and clacked, clopped and clanged his way around De Coursey Square, delivering several creamy, rich milk bottles for all the thirsty mouths.

His grandmother had limitless energy. After a lifetime spent raising eleven children she missed the endless demands on her. So whenever possible she thrived on the opportunity to cook, clean, talk, shout, and, with matriarchal authority, grill her multitude of hyperactive active grandchildren on whether they had said their daily prayers. Regardless of the time of night she'd finally lay her head down, or how terrible the weather conditions, off she'd religiously march every morning to six o'clock morning mass. She harbored a bitter resentment against Pope John Paul XXIII for his scandalous modernization of the Catholic Church. She viewed as particularly blasphemous, his allowing the Mass to be said in English instead of Latin, while turning the altar around so the priest faced the congregation was almost as equally troublesome for her. She was further scandalized by the Pope allowing Catholics to attend Sunday mass on Saturdays. It was impossible to attend Sunday mass on a Saturday. She also had no doubt those changing to the Saturday mass would be found guilty of committing venial if not necessarily mortal sins. They should have known better. Although unquestioning of the Pope's infallibility on all doctrinal matters, his grandmother remained deeply troubled by the liberal direction her beloved church was taking under this misguided pope. He was so old, God bless him, he should have been praying for a happy death rather than destroying the holy, Roman, and Apostolic church that had done fine thank you very much for almost two thousand years!

Supposedly stone deaf, she possessed an uncanny ability to hear what she shouldn't. When Murphy asked her one day in the kitchen where she wanted to be buried, her grumpy son Joe, the only unmarried one, muttered quietly into his Irish Press newspaper, so low that Murphy could barely make out what he was saying, "She'll be put somewhere, anywhere in Glasnevin cemetery." Whereupon his grandmother turned on Joe with fury and roared, "I will not indeed, I'll be buried down in Kildare beside your father so I will." And so, in time, she was. This diminutive old lady was not to be trifled with.

Despite producing twelve children anything related to sex was strictly forbidden in her home. She viewed England and anything remotely connected with that evil place, as intractably linked with sin, meaning of course, illicit sexual activity. Their filthy newspapers, three of which she religiously purchased every Sunday after mass, were abundant confirmation of that.

She abhorred anything to do with that depraved, pagan land and regularly reminded Murphy that the Irish had a body of laws in place before the Sassenach had even learned to walk upright. "And Stonehenge!" she'd roar indignantly. "Sure, Newgrange in Kildare is far better built, let's in much more light on Solstice day, and," waving a dismissive hand, "tis over one thousand years older than that place over there that's falling apart! If they built a block of corporation houses around it, t'would improve the look."

It was tragic the English ruling class had for centuries

systematically destroyed the Irish nation and culture. She was convinced the damage continued nowadays because the road to hell began on the planks that led generations of Irish boys and girls, herded like cattle to the boats leaving from DunLaoire, across the Irish sea to Wales, then to London town where generations of previously pure Irish had lost their religion and their Irishness to that Godless, Saxon society and their filthy, immoral way of life. After even a week in London they'd return home to their confused parents with piercing Cockney accents, weighed down with boxes of illegal condoms and hostile attitudes.

Interestingly, on the first morning of that Christmas when his Aunt Pearl was making up her mother's bed, she was shocked to discover a copy of DH Lawrence's Lady Chatterley's Lover hidden under the mattress. When confronted, Murphy's embarrassed grandmother first became flustered then furiously disavowed any knowledge of its existence and demanded to immediately know who had brought such disgusting filth into her Catholic Irish home.

Retreating hastily to the safer ground her kitchen offered, she quickly cooked up breakfast then went upstairs to the men's bedroom where her eldest son, Murphy's father, was hiding under the covers painfully dealing with his hangover. Now safe, Murphy had just crawled back into the same bed, when his grandmother came barreling through the door armed with a large glass of whiskey along with a steaming plate piled high with rashers, sausages, tomatoes, beans, black pudding, and eggs. His father turned chalk white but even at age fifty-five he remained his mother's son and silently accepted the plate. He struggled to sit up and eat while being silently observed by his mother's eagle eye. His lack of appetite prompted her to wonder if her quality of cooking was finally failing her. Her successful son, usually so commanding in his daily business life, reverted to childhood, and ate silently without question. While his mother looked out the window to see what the neighbors were up to, he managed to momentarily distract her while pouring much of the whiskey into a nearby flowerpot. Observing the already half empty glass, his mother, who had never once touched a drop of alcohol in her life, assumed her son must be especially thirsty and quickly went downstairs before returning with a full refill.

On the second evening of that Christmas visit, Murphy joined the men and his boy cousins in the packed front room, away from the women who were busy preparing food in the kitchen while enjoying glasses of sherry.

An enthusiastic sing song erupted and soon booming men's voices threatened the house foundations with a variety of old Irish songs, Moore's melodies, selections from My Fair Lady, The Pirates of Penance and, for the more adventurous, a taste of Mario Lanza.

Everybody was in great form, and empty Guinness and Power's whiskey bottles quickly piled up as the nine brothers razed each other fiercely about their childhood years in this humble house. As children, life was tough. None of them had known new clothes, each one wearing hand-me-downs from the brother above him, yet now here they were part of the newly evolving Irish middle class all smartly turned out, successful men of the world.

Murphy noticed his father, with a nearly disguised smile of satisfaction, take one of many photos his mother kept of her sons on the mantelpiece and show it to the others. It was an Irish Times photo of himself and his brother at an annual general meeting of the successful publicly traded company they ran. He had every right to be proud.

"Hey, Murphy, Chris, get some more Guinness from the kitchen, will ye, lads?"

"Sure, Uncle," Murphy had no idea which one had spoken but knew they were all thirsty men and there must never be a shortage of the brew. Chris and he went off at a gallop.

In the kitchen, the women, with pursed lips and frowns, loaded them up then turned back to their work and glasses of sherry.

The bottles clanked in the boys' arms. They were calling to Murphy, beginning what would a deadly lifelong obsession.

"Let's try one. They'll never miss it," he hissed.

"The job is Oxo," Chris agreed.

They dashed towards the bathroom, locked the door, and within moments had each opened a bottle. Murphy had occasionally stolen sips from various glasses before but the drink had never tasted good and he couldn't understand why grown people liked it so much. This time however was different and, as the frothy black liquid poured down his throat, a magical transformation grew over him; a light headedness and sense of ease that made him giggle at clever statements he made. Chris began to laugh too and fearful of being caught they fervently shushed each other then collapsed onto the floor and rolled about with the hilarity of it all.

"Who's in there?" A pounding rattled the door. "Come out now. I need to go. NOW!"

Momentarily sobered, they recognized Uncle Joe's voice, gathered the bottles, and bolted out as quickly as he bolted in.

Nobody noticed their befuddled states when they delivered the remaining bottles. "Is that all they sent us? Jayzaz, a bird never flew on one wing. Back with you boys, and bring us a decent few more, a dozen at least," ordered another uncle.

And away they scampered, stopping again on the way back for more nourishment for themselves.

By the time, Murphy had downed a second bottle he was happier than he'd imagined possible. Although he had a terrible singing voice and knew only some of the lyrics, he enthusiastically joined in the singing and rejoiced in the company of these mighty men all having a great craic together.

"Come for dinner!" announced his mother her head partially in the door.

Furious at her for ruining the moment, Murphy shouted, "Get away to hell and leave us alone. We aren't hungry. And we don't want food, we're drinkin!"

His wisdom was confirmed by the approving roars of laughter from his fellow men.

His startled mother, after recovering from the initial shock that rendered her motionless, leaped forward, grasped his arm, and dragged him screaming down the hallway.

His world began to spin. He felt horribly sick. Closing his eyes to make it go away only made it worse.

His mother abruptly stopped studied him. "My God, you've been drinking. You reek of porter!"

She'd hardly issued those words when he heaved two bottles of Guinness all over her elegant party dress. Then he started to bawl from misery and shame of how he'd spoken to her and the inevitable consequences it would bring.

She took him to the bathroom, scrubbed him off then sent him straight to bed where he lay for a long time being sucked into a whirlpool every time he shut his eyes. He passionately swore he would never go through that again but, later, when the bad feelings wore off, he fondly remembered those carefree moments when life had briefly seemed so wonderful. That was surely a feeling to treasure.

He wasn't sure if it was a dream but later when falling in and out of sleep, Murphy felt his parents stand over him. His mother's accusing voice shouted bitterly complaining. "Your women I put up with but I'll not have you making a drunk of my son!"

His father's response was, as always, calm. "Shur

t'was only a little drink. No real harm was done, was it?"

Perhaps not then, but it was a precursor of future dark times.

A highlight of the Dublin adventure was meeting his favorite uncle. His mother's brother Paddy lived and worked in Dublin. All Murphy remembered of that grandmother was hearing her once comment that she had married down when she wed his grandfather. Perhaps that was the origin of his mother saying at the drop of a hat whenever family was discussed, "Did I mention my mother was educated on the continent by the nuns?" This was always delivered in a casual, throwaway tone, suggesting it meant absolutely nothing to her, but everyone knew you had to come from a certain class in society to have a daughter being educated on the continent, and in France no less. His grandfather was a civil servant. He died when Murphy was very young so they never met. The only image available was a photograph of an old, gaunt looking man with gray hair and a gloomy "life is not to be enjoyed" face. Murphy's mother claimed he held a senior management position in the Irish civil service. It wasn't until later that Murphy discovered his grandfather had spent all his working life pedaling around Dublin's city streets on his bicycle delivering the post. An honorable calling no doubt, but not quite the lofty position portrayed by his mother. In later years Murphy would smile when thinking of his mother's innate sense of Irish peasant snobbery, a national obsession, where a penny always smugly looked down on a half penny.

Unlike his father, uncle Paddy was a civil servant who spent each excruciating day of his working life working in the government's statistics office and hating every second it. Murphy had heard him telling mother how he, an unreligious man, was forced every day, along with the rest of the office clerks, to get down on his knees and say the rosary. The prayers were led by his department head, a spindly bachelor who eternally regretted not having become a priest and who lived with his mother who never forgave him for not being one.

Uncle Paddy's real love was the army. He served for many years in the reserves, and would joyfully have joined up fulltime except for the fact that he had to mind his mother since both her daughters had married.

As was their tradition, he took the children to see the pantomime at the Gaiety Theater. That year it was Mother Goose. On previous years, they'd seen Hansel and Gretel and The Pied Piper among others but Murphy thought, as he always did, this year was surely the best as he joined hundreds of screaming children shouting warnings at the good person when the baddie was about to attack. "Watch out behind you!!!" they all roared with frenetic concern. The goody looked out into the audience and innocently asked, "Wha? Watch out for wha?" The stupidity of that drove them into a collective frenzy at which they arose in unison, waved frantically and screamed even more vociferously, "Behind, look behind ye! Ye egit!" Fortunately, at the last possible moment the goody did turn, vanquish the baddie, and all was well with the world.

After the panto they spilled out into the streets and uncle Paddy took them first for fish & chips to Fortes Italian chipper on O'Connell Street, then over to Moore Street lined with treasures of a magical kind where hawkers shouted the magnificence of their wares.

First Murphy bought sheet music for a popular song when guaranteed he'd be able to sing almost as Bobby Darrin did on the record. Then he was drawn to sparks flying from the hand of a vendor.

"How long does it last, Sir?" he politely asked.

"How long wud ya like it te last?"

"Five minutes or longer please."

"Den dats how long it'll be." Murphy bought six.

The hawker silently thanked the almighty for culchies and smiled pleasantly as he took the shilling from the child's outstretched palm. Later that night the best of the sparklers lasted less than thirty seconds.

All too quickly their precious few days in the big city were over. December the 23rd had quickly come and t'was time to return to Limerick. Leaving that special house of his Christmas childhood was always difficult. After the excitement of the previous days and evenings filled with mighty craic, laughter, music, singing, occasional arguments, children rushing untamed all over the house, slowing down only when exhaustion overcame them, Murphy always felt empty, a full sail suddenly without wind, as they prepared for departure.

Watching his granny standing stone like at the front door, Murphy watched as a dark cloud of sadness settled over the house. "Can't ye stay just a little bit longer?" she begged his father, sounding more like a beggar for loose change than a matriarch who had once unquestioningly ruled the roost. This was their ritual and it never failed to sadden him. Even though still a child, he instinctively felt his beloved grandmother's sense of loneliness. She had lived in this home for all her married life, had raised a large family in a house with barely room to swing a cat let alone twelve children. Providing for them had been her reason for living but now they were gone from her. Only her cranky bachelor son remained and even he was out of the house most of the time. Murphy reasoned the sound of silence in her home must now be deafening.

His father again patiently explained they had to be on their way. As they drove away from De Coursey Square, the look of sadness on his grandmother's old, wrinkled face bothered him. But she was quickly gone from his sight then mind as he found himself wondering what special presents Santa would soon be leaving for him under the Christmas tree in Limerick.

Chapter Eight

CHRISTMAS IN LIMERICK

The fun continued after arriving home. Still full of the action-packed days at his grandmother's, partying with his numerous cousins and soaking in the vibrancy of the packed Dublin streets, now on Christmas Eve Murphy felt the excitement of charging down O'Connell Street for some last-minute gift shopping. He happily toddled along in his mother's wake first into Todds, then Cannocks, then on to Roches Stores.

She also took him to see Santa Claus. His brother and sister refused to go claiming they were too old. Grainne scorned Murphy for being a baby, but he didn't care what the Wicked Witch said. He always loved talking to Santa and, equally special, having his mother all to himself, if only for a while.

One aspect about Santa that puzzled Murphy was his ability to simultaneously be in so many stores. True, when they left one store Santa would have just about enough time to move on to the next. But he often looked different, was fatter or skinnier, taller, or shorter than before. Sometimes he'd be full of laughter and energy while reeking of beer or whiskey at one place, then have absolutely no smell and be quite reserved, almost bored, at the next. It was very strange if you thought about it enough, but he always spoke with a thick Limerick accent, and with that consolation Murphy accepted the mystery.

With shopping done, excusing their way through even more crowds, they walked up William Street and stopped at the Golden Grill for some steaming hot fresh fish with mushy peas and the best chips in the world. One man who worked there had once been on the Late Late TV show displaying his skill at cutting spuds at an alarming speed. Murphy had watched fascinated, guiltily hoping to see a finger or two and lots of blood suddenly shoot into the big basin of freshly cut chips.

Murphy loved those rare occasions when his mother and he were alone on these expeditions. That Christmas was no exception. He relished having her all to himself as they sat enjoying their feast. Stealing a quick glance, Murphy thought his mother looked so beautiful, regally elegant, and obviously happy to be with him, her cheeks glowing as they chatted. Sometimes she'd take his hand in hers across the table then pause briefly, looking deeply into him, and softly calling him Lovey or her little man. Murphy realized in those rare moments that, despite everything, she really did love him and that undoubtedly, he was her favorite child.

Swaggering back down William Street he happily squeezed her hand never wanting to let go of the moment, but eventually they staggered down the Avenue and in the door laden with their numerous packages. His uncle Frank had already arrived from the farm in Kildare to deliver the annual Christmas turkey, a goose, a side of ham, and a sack bulging with fresh spuds dug minutes before he left, with the clay still dangling off them.

After dinner, his mother and Grainne began to prepare the banquet for the neighbors who would later drop in for music, food, and craic. Large blue plates with Celtic patterns were heaped high with beautiful ham. There was brown soda bread baked by his aunt Pearl's hands, so fresh it crumbled when touched, and covered with rich butter she'd made. Lashings of thick cream, also from the farm, graced the surface of Irish coffees in Waterford Crystal glasses that only adults could touch. There was also whiskey for the men. Endless bottles of Guinness stout and Harp lager sat on a white cloth-covered table waiting for the young men to open them. Alongside was Harveys Bristol Cream sherry for the ladies, and sparkling O'Sullivan's red lemonade for the children.

Before the party, they had to attend Christmas mass. Occasionally, they'd go to the Redemptorist church, but this year they went down O'Connell to the Jesuit church, first passing St. Joseph's on the right where his brother and sister had already been confirmed by the Bishop while promising to renounce the devil and all his evil ways.

They knew most of the people at church, muffled up in their finest winter coats, and enjoyed singing along when the choir led the congregation in songs that rejoiced in the birth of the savior.

Mass over, it seemed the whole Avenue passed through Sutton that Christmas Eve. Even the two Protestant families came by for a brief visit. The smell of hundreds of sausages greeted guests as they came through the open front door. His father had brought a big supply of Haffner's sausages down from Dublin and they would be served last. And there was drink, rivers of it. Excited faces shouted to be heard. His mother went around smiling at every guest, and making sure everyone had enough to eat and drink. From the heaped plates, Murphy knew everybody had all saved their appetites to enjoy his mother's cooking. He felt proud of her excellent reputation for catering a party.

Music and song were enjoyed by all. People were called on to do their party piece, play the piano, sing a ditty, recite a poem, tell a joke, whatever it was; everybody had to perform something. Some made everybody laugh; others brought tears to the eye. His father held a song well and sang one called, "Maire My Love." Murphy wished it was for his mother but wasn't sure.

After the party pieces were done the fiddlers and

banjo players struck up and music rose to the heavens. Dancing began. Feet beat the floor with increasing pace as the young men swung their partners around faster and faster. His father was out there too, flushed and handsome, squiring the prettiest of the ladies, whispering in their ears and squeezing them tightly around their waists, stepping out with the best of them. His mother stood in the shadows watching. For a while one foot tapped longingly, then it stopped and the only thing that moved on her was the glass traveling regularly to her lips.

But the beat and the merriment filled Murphy with excitement so he could think of nothing else. All the children, kneeling in the corner, lapped it up, elbowing each other's sides, giggling, sniggering with hands over their mouths, laughing at the silly adult behavior.

Around ten o clock, and way past Murphy's usual bedtime, his mother came in with steaming platefuls of Haffners sausages and tomato sauce so delicious his mouth watered for more even after his belly was stuffed. Their arrival was the sign for the children of the Avenue to be taken home by the teenagers so they'd be in bed and well asleep before Santa arrived. Murphy's annual concern about Santa being burned alive in a chimney sizzling with heat from a roaring turf fire, and Murphy being somehow blamed for it, fortunately never came to anything.

After lying in bed tossing and turning for what seemed an eternity, he finally drifted off with the sound of wild laughter and dizzying music ringing in his ears.

Next day, when anyone mentioned how grand the party was, his mother feigned collapse and swore, as she had every Christmas since Murphy could remember, "I'll never do it again; shur it's far too exhausting."

And she wouldn't, until the following year.

Chapter Nine

KILKEE

Kilkee is a small town in west county Clare. Three thousand souls lived there, except in summertime when hordes of Limerick people descended on Limerick By The Sea. Then lodging and guest houses, small hotels, and the caravan park, all overflowed. The town hangs precariously on the edge of Europe, with America the next place west of it. The strand used to be called New York View.

Kilkee Bay is a magnificent horseshoe of golden sand partially surrounded by dramatic cliffs and constantly subject to a thousand daily moods, depending on the light. It lies at the point where land turns to sand in the far west of Ireland and it is there, in the bay, that tides make sprat, mackerel, rockfish, jellyfish, and lobster, dart, weave, and float beneath the surface, mixing in fluid dance with a thousand variations of swaying seaweed. Echoes of ancient rock grumble on the ocean floor, resurrecting the eerie rhythm and music of deep down things, while the cliffs protect as best they can against the ever-threatening anger of the Atlantic Ocean.

The family summer home was in the east end of town. Murphy's father always stayed in Limerick until Friday night. He'd then spend the weekend at the golf club which was close by the cliff face that fell over a hundred feet into the crashing, swirling waves. George's Head was farther over. Whenever cows wandered early morning up towards the top, everyone knew it would rain later that day. If anyone walked to the top of George's Head they'd notice not a tree nor bush in sight, but the effort was well worth it for the spectacular views of the Loop Head peninsula and Bishop's Island. On a clear day, it was possible to see the Twelve Bens Mountains in Galway and even the Arran islands.

Below George's head rests Byrne's Cove, a swimming place where only men were allowed. It was a favorite place for priests who liked to swim then lie naked under the warm sun. If women came within an ass's roar, they'd be shooed away. But all boys and men were welcomed.

On the other side of the bay lay the Pollock Holes. These were three separate, deep holes that reached out for a mile or so under the ocean like fingers trying to touch eternity. When the tide was out, the water in the Pollock holes was clean and silent, making it easy to see every movement of life below the surface. Cascades of fresh seawater filled the pools after every tide, nurturing the exotic vegetation and wide variety of shellfish, especially crabs, which scurried unseen except for the motion of quivering waters. Thousands of wee, black, yellow-tailed fish darted frantically, one blindly following the other, moving in perfect harmony and fascinating the children every year.

On arriving that summer of his fourteenth birthday, Murphy looked for familiar faces and they were not hard to find. Old, usually toothless local women were selling periwinkles and dilisk from stalls along the wall that stretched the length of the bay. The donkey that brought the cart was being rented out on the beach, two bob for one ride up and down the sands. Already he recognized a couple of the lads from school, wearing swimming trunks and carrying towels under their arms, strolling along the strand.

Each of the children in Murphy's family had their own room and after putting his stuff away Murphy headed out to see who was around. Almost immediately he banged into school mates Pecker Gallivan, Rashers O'Brian, and Spud Murphy.

The first few days were spent quietly. They'd be in

Kilkee for two months so there was no need to rush anything. Ray Charles sang "Summertime" on the radio, and the living really was easy. The weather favored them before the cows began to move up George's Head and they used the first week to ease their way into summer. They only woke when the sun roused them with its heat, then they'd spend a long time silently drinking steaming cups of tea while munching on rice crispies and looking along the strand to see what life was there. They'd take leisurely morning swims or ramble over to the Pollock holes and, if it was a warm afternoon, they'd do some fishing, or play a round of golf, before hopping over the wall for the dinner Mary, a local girl who helped Murphy's mother, prepared each night around six o' clock.

While most of Murphy's school friends owned homes in Kilkee, people from all of Limerick's social classes visited for the summer holidays. The workers came for two weeks, usually in June. Murphy and his friends would arrive early that month and, unless visiting the farm, Murphy would usually stay until late summer when it was time to return to school. By the end of July most people had returned to Limerick and by then, with the tourist season winding down and many of the local men having returned to work at London's building sites, it was like having their own private playground.

Within a week of arriving this time, Murphy's uncomplicated life was forever changed when Pecker reminded him about the racket tournament. They played this game with tennis rackets and balls, which they belted against the alley wall and the other person slammed back. If the ball bounced more than once, or went outside the line drawn in the sand, you'd lose the point. There were twenty-one points in each game. Best of three games won. Pecker's Dad was usually the umpire. No arguing with him no matter how wrong he was. Those were the rules and they were never questioned. Usually a local lad would win. Often it was one of the DeLucia boys whose family owned the local chipper. The women in the mixed matches were expected to stay out of the way and only hit the ball in an emergency.

Murphy played well in the singles, and made it to the quarterfinals. Then he played Tom Nolan, son of the local doctor who, like Murphy, was fourteen. He'd known him since early childhood. There were always people sitting on the alley wall watching the games and, during a break, Murphy looked up and noticed a beautiful girl up there. She was about thirteen or fourteen years old, had a wonderful smile and, interestingly, she was looking directly at Murphy. She had a dark complexion, eyes shining brightly like clear mountain lakes inviting him to happily drown in them. She wore a yellow top and dark blue shorts that went down to her knees. Rich, black, overflowing hair danced all around her face as she swayed and the sea wind blew it around her shoulders with wisps of it touching full, red lips that should have been outlawed for the temptation they offered.

Murphy had been leading Tom by one game to zero and leading fifteen to four in the second set. But then he saw her smiling warmly down at him, her bronzed legs swinging enticingly back and forth, head tipped at a slight angle. Running around he still managed to see fleeting images of her and heard snatches of her laughter. He began flexing his athletic muscles to impress her and, shamefully, began to show off this athleticism by hitting the ball even harder. That strategy completely backfired and he lost the second game before returning to sanity and easily winning the third.

After shaking hands with Tom, he wiped his dripping forehead and snuck a peek through his towel to see if the girl was still up there. She was! She was! It was then that he had a crazy thought. He'd been thinking of asking a girl out on a date for a while now. None of the other lads had done it yet, but somebody eventually would. Damn it to hell, he'd be the one to do it! He'd ask her out, just like that, but casually in case she said no. And even if she agreed, he wouldn't tell a soul about it, not the lads, nor anyone at home, especially nobody at home.

He walked up the stone steps to the top of the alley walls. It took a lifetime. He sneaked a look and saw she was watching his ascent. His heart pounded loudly, ready to explode, while butterflies danced a wild gig in his stomach. The girl helped by smiling and saying, "You play well," or something like that. He saw rather than heard her blood red lips moving and out came words with a northern accent.

'Now you fool, ask her out now, you idjit you!' a voice in his head instructed him. "So, do you have any interest in going to a flick?" stumbled out of his mouth.

"What's playing?" she said.

"Elvis in Blue Hawaii," said Murphy, being very cool. She looked at him in a queer way and said nothing. This was terrible. Years passed while he waited for a response. Luckily none of the lads were around. What sort of an idjit was he to put himself into this ridiculous situation?

He was about to do a runner when the girl said, "Ay, that'd be lovely. What's yuer name? I'm Ann, Ann Lamont, from Belfast."

"Grand. So, I'll see you outside the Arcadia at five past eight."

"But it usually starts at eight," said the suddenly wonderful Ann Lamont from Belfast. "By the way, you never told me your name."

"Oh yeah, it's Murphy. I can't get there till after eight." He lied, although it wasn't completely an untruth. He really couldn't turn up before eight. If he did, the Lads would see him and really take the Mick. He'd have to wait until the cinema was dark, so they could sneak in unnoticed.

"What's your name?" said he, now looking directly at her eyes.

"Already told you, Ann, Ann Lamont."

She must have thought he was an idiot. But he was lost in her beauty, her mysterious femininity; was fascinated by how her soft voice lilted and danced as she spoke. Her hand then reached out for his in a formal introduction. Her touch made Murphy tingle, feel strange, all weird inside.

"Grand. I'll see you at the Arcadia later." Then he walked off, doubtless leaving the lovely Ann somewhat puzzled. He would again disappoint her later that same evening.

Dinner took forever that night. Brother Liam wanted to come with him to the film. "I'm going with some of the lads." Murphy abruptly rejected him. Fortunately, nobody noticed his face was redder than the previous night's blazing sunset. The tapestry of lies continued. He had told the lads he was going to play a few holes of golf with Liam before it got dark and wouldn't be going out that night. This dating game was becoming much more complicated than what, at the time, had seemed a simple idea. "Eat up, child, you haven't had a thing," his concerned mother said pointing to the untouched salmon, peas and spuds lying on his plate. "I'm not hungry, thanks," as he pushed his plate away. Usually he ate like a horse so his mother was concerned and checked his forehead for fever. "Are you getting sick, Lovey?" This produced an impatient shake of the head from her young son.

Mary came in and cleared away his plate. Excusing himself from the table, he went to the bathroom. Now that the meeting would soon happen, his afternoon confidence vanished. He wondered what would happen? What was expected of him? What was he to do? Should he kiss her, perhaps try, and touch her breasts? And if so, what then? How far to go or not go? Back came the dreaded butterflies doing another variation of the previous jigs in his stomach. He spent ages sitting on the cold toilet seat trying to poop but, after several loud farts, reluctantly gave up. It was a false alarm. He then thoroughly bathed himself making sure he smelled of Palmolive soap all over his trembling body. While vigorously brushing his teeth, he came close to scraping off the enamel as the radio jingle, "You'll wonder where the yellow went when you brush your teeth with Pepsodent," kept repeating itself in his head. Then he plastered his hair with Brylcream. It bolstered his fragile confidence to imagine he looked something like Ricky Nelson or Cliff Richard, hair slicked and combed back with a parting down the right-hand side. Not sure what to wear he came close to asking his sister but wisely decided against that so he simply threw on blue jeans and a stylish, wild colored shirt his father had brought him back from Carnaby Street in London. His sister viewed him suspiciously as he tried to leave the house without being closely observed. "Good luck, see you later," he yelled and left as fast as possible, banging the door, while feeling his sister's eyes scorched into his back.

At a quarter to eight he'd strategically positioned himself, hiding behind Burkes butcher's wall. It was about fifty yards from the Arcadia Film Theater. Sure enough, at ten to eight along came the lads, all of them talking at once. Hands were flying in all directions with no one listening to anyone else as usual. Pecker Gallivan, Rashers O'Brien, and Spud Murphy walked into the Arcadia. He had carefully planned not to be waiting for Ann outside that theater with those lads lurking around to ridicule him.

"How's id goin?" a Kilkee voice asked his ear. Horrible breath engulfed him. He turned to find Jerry Burke's ugly face inches from his. Burke had mountains of pimples waiting to explode. His father owned the butcher shop. He worked behind the counter and helped kill the cows. He was thick as two planks and nosey to boot. He was legitimately wondering what the hell Murphy was doing hiding behind their wall. "How's ie goin?" he asked again with a greater sense of urgency, his bullfrog eyes bulging. T'was said he was a bit away in the head,

Murphy ignored him, casually straightened up, dusted off his hands and said, "Well, I'm off, good luck." He left young Burke frowning, scratching his arse with one hand and scraping his pimples with the other, trying to figure out what Murphy was doing hiding behind their business wall.

Heading up the street in the opposite direction to the theater, Murphy could feel Jerry Burke's eyes suspiciously following, watching his every step. Once out of sight, he cut across O'Curry Street, doubled back around by the seafront then down a side lane to the Arcadia, now running quickly because it was past eight o'clock. Moments later the lovely Ann Lamont arrived looking gorgeous and happy, wearing a sparkling smile, white short sleeved blouse and blue mini skirt that ended well above her knees.

'I've done it,' he thought excitedly. 'I'm on an official date. Fair play, boy!'

"You're here," Sherlock brilliantly observed feeling relieved and supremely pleased.

"Aye. "

That lovely lilting voice and smile sent warm currents of strange energy racing through his body. Suddenly the world was a wonderful place. He couldn't understand what he'd been worried about. Now Ann took his hand. He quickly looked around to see if anyone was watching, but no, the coast was clear. Then, with horror, he suddenly felt movement between his legs. He'd done nothing to encourage it so It must have automatically happened when Ann took his hand. He'd have to soon endure yet another embarrassing confession. Oh, sweet Jesus, not now please! Unfortunately, God was busy somewhere else, because it got worse. His pants had become skin tight and he was no longer able to breathe, practically suffocating. He was terrified Ann might have noticed his discomfort and would walk off leaving him alone at the ticket counter. Turning away, he bought the tickets, opened the door of the theater, and moved Ann quickly inside to the welcoming darkness. His problem had gone, at least for the moment, and Ann was still smiling.

The balcony was full, as were most of the rear seats. Murphy wanted to stay far from the lads. He knew exactly where they were because Pecker Gallivan had a laugh like a demented horse. The lads were near the back on the right side. Hastily, he marched Ann down to midway along the left-hand side, safely away from them. After the ads finished, Blue Hawaii began and Elvis smirked out from the screen before beginning his crooning. Murphy cautiously made his move and strategically lifted his left arm to put it around Ann's shoulder. Unfortunately, there was some interference from the big person behind who cursed him for it, drawing unwelcome attention. He pretended to be stretching but was immediately asked to stop blocking the view.

After Elvis had, for some reason Murphy couldn't grasp, burst into song three more times, he finally summoned up the courage to again get his arm in motion. It took several awkward attempts and many a time he almost did it, but froze at the last moment. Ann tried to rescue him by moving closer and taking his other hand in hers. Eternal minutes later while he was contemplating his next strategic move Ann snuggled closer and laid her head on his shoulder. This unexpected move confused him. He was supposed to be in charge. Clearly out of his depth, he began to panic wondering what it was she expected from him. Pretending to casually glance around he sneaked a hasty peep down her blouse that was majestically moving in and out, rising and falling as she breathed. Her nipples peeked out and winked up invitingly at him. She caught him looking and smiled warmly, but Murphy almost died from the embarrassment of being caught.

Meanwhile, Elvis was aimlessly wandering along the beach, strumming a Hawaiian guitar, smiling at dozens of beautiful women dressed in grass skirts and skimpy tops, who swayed their slender waists as they adoringly looked back at him. Despite their worship, Elvis still managed to look as confused as Murphy felt.

The film had been on for over an hour and he decided he'd have to kiss Ann. From what he'd observed so far, she was raring to go. Besides, Protestant girls were supposed to be real terrors what with no sins or confessions in their religion to worry about. One of his aunts firmly maintained that a religion without guilt isn't worth a tinker's curse.

Murphy moved his hand from Ann's left shoulder to turn her cheek over near his then kiss her on the lips. He didn't really care if he missed a little, anywhere close to her mouth would do. If he got lucky she might allow him to drop the hand outside her blouse. He'd heard from reliable sources that sometimes you'd be allowed to open the girl's blouse. Older lads at school who had done it wouldn't wash that hand for ages. Most the boys were left with minds running wild trying to imagine the reality of touching a girl like that. Most girls got kissed on a first date. It was expected from the boy. Murphy was about to make his move when a terrible tingling began in the arm he had around Ann's shoulder. It quickly got worse and hurt like mad while Elvis still found reasons to sing another bunch of songs. Within minutes Murphy's entire left arm was in agony with pins and needles. He could have simply excused himself to go to the toilets, but instead stoically sat paralyzed beside this lovely girl.

A smirking Elvis jolted Murphy back to the present as he sang one final song. Murphy promised himself he'd take Ann to the shelter near the golf course and at the very least, drop the hand. Jesus, it'd be magic to finally feel the real thing, touch someone else's flesh for a change. To finally touch a live girl and not a fantasy. Even though his left arm was now fully paralyzed, he was getting hard below again. Well, right then, he didn't care if he did go to hell.

The film mercifully ended with Elvis sailing off into a

golden sunset with his girl while Murphy hadn't come close to kissing his. The lights came up and he looked around. The lads were sitting up, elbowing each other, unable to say anything as they gawked at Murphy's arm possessively around Ann. Suddenly he understood. He was one up on them - was the first to have a real date with a girl. The throbbing in his arm and side disappeared and he found a swagger in his stride. Taking Ann's hand in his, as they walked out, he gave the lads a curt nod as if barely aware of their existence. "Lads, how's it going?" he casually threw out as if used to having a beautiful girl on his arm every day of the week.

Murphy and Ann walked hand in hand to DeLucia's chipper. Ann got them a table while he went up to place their order. Just then the lads rushed breathlessly in. Pecker Gallivan shuffled up to the counter. "You could have told us," he said resentfully, shaking his head.

"Just didn't want any messing from you lot. Anyway, come over and meet the bird."

Murphy introduced the lads then turned away from them. After finishing the nosh, he wished them good luck and, behind Ann's back, returned their enthusiastic winking and waltzed Miss Lamont out the door. Now began the delicate part of the mission.

Anne's family had rented a house out near Murphy's place by the golf course. It was a decent walk along the path by the strand lit by a rich June moon. The Atlantic was unusually calm. They could see the Pollock Holes on the left and George's Head to the right at the end of the bay. They held hands and breathed in the sea, seaweed, dillisk, and the salty air. He asked Ann about her life in Belfast. "It's lovely and quiet there. Are you Catholic or Protestant?" she asked. It turned out she was Protestant. He'd never spoken to a Protestant girl before and there he was with one on his first date. Magic! They were supposed to be hot stuff, what with no sins or confessions to worry about. This could easily lead to something wild. Finally, after years of frustrating, yet highly imaginative fantasizing, he was about to experience a live "occasion of sin" and could proudly boast about it to the priest at his next confession. And he didn't give a tinker's curse about the penance, in fact, he hoped for the worst.

"My Daddy's a doctor and so was Mum before we came along so she had to stop working and be a Mammy." Murphy's mother would approve. Two doctors in the family, even if they were Protestant. Ann had two brothers and she went to an all girl's school. "I don't have a boyfriend now," she added, gently squeezing his hand as she said this.

It's a good sign, Murphy thought as they walked along the Atlantic road up by the golf links. The shelter was on their left. He was about to walk them over there to court, but at the last moment froze, he couldn't do it.

Suddenly they were outside her house. He looked into Ann's smiling eyes. She was wonderful. There was a come-hither look reaching out from her. And she wasn't Catholic! He desperately wanted to touch her impurely and finally turn his impure thoughts of the past few years into impure actions. Only the devil himself knew what other charms she might have hidden and waiting for him to explore.

Then with no warning, another great wave if shyness turned him to stone. If only he could be Elvis for a minute, just to get the thing started, and then change back to being himself once they'd begun kissing. Clever words formed in his brain but failed to make the journey out of his mouth. His body had become a ton weight, his feet cemented into the ground. His arms didn't respond when he tried to reach out. He was unable to move any limb, couldn't even speak. Sexual desire had been replaced by a need to take Ann into his arms, and profusely apologize for his inadequacy. An awkward silence followed as Anne waited for him to make the first move. Her skirt was blown open by the late-night breeze and peeled back slowly across her thigh. For a moment, he saw her white panties. Ann shuffled her feet, smiling less as she became impatient before looking away again. Below them in the Bay, came the cries of the last seagulls returning as the swirling Atlantic wind brought them effortlessly gliding home. Seconds became minutes. By now, Murphy wanted to be a thousand miles away. He decided to do a runner. Feeling cowardly and inept, he took Ann's hand in his, politely shook it, said, "Goodnight," then took off into the night.

Along the promenade, he ran into the lads, who were gasping to hear all the details of his conquest. "Did you drop the hand?" "Did she allow the tongue?" "How far did ye get?" The innocents clamored for details as they stood back in frenzied anticipation and in complete awe. Pausing reflectively Murphy, now the wily veteran, stifled a bored yawn. "Drop the hand my arse, sure that's nothing." He laughed contemptuously, dismissing the notion with a wave of his hand. "She's a hot piece all right, a cracker, mad for it. Loved it. Sure, you can spot them a mile off. Besides, she's a Prod." He laughed, head skyward waving to the sparkling stars that had smiled favorably down on him that night.

On that special night, as he listened to the sounds of lover's laughter drifting on the gentle Atlantic wind which mixed all before it with divine alchemy, Murphy was rich with the knowledgeable air of one who has done battle, seen it all, damn it, and survived to tell the tale. Who better than he to know? The lads understood he was now a hard case, a ladies' man. The first of them to take a girl out on a real date! They were seriously impressed about how far he'd got. They looked at him in awe as if he'd scored the winning Triple Crown try for Ireland.

Not a word was said as the lads rambled home with heads down, hands in pockets, lost in private thoughts about the unfolded mystery.

Murphy broke away to make his own way home. Everything was quiet now except for the sound of the waves landing on the beach, and occasional laughter drifting across the Bay. Car lights pointed into the ocean at George's Head, before lovers turned them off, and the groping began.

Murphy's sandals made wet prints in the sand as he felt a bubble burst inside. He was alone now, no more need for pretense, and feeling both happy and sad. Happy because he'd done the dreaded first date, but sad he was too shy and funked kissing Ann. He was also ashamed that he'd thrashed her in front of the lads.

Next morning, he decided to ask her out again. But he didn't, and they never had another conversation. Instead, any time he saw the lovely Ann Lamont walking towards him, he hastily crossed the road to avoid her. Making matters worse, he completely ignored her for the remainder of that confusing summer of his fourteenth year.

Chapter Ten

CONFESSION

From the ceiling of the golden domed church, Jesus Christ, the Virgin Mary, Saint Patrick, Saint Ignatius, and several angels with flapping wings frowned down on the sinners who kneeled motionless with heads bowed, hands tightly clasped in prayer. Sunlight shone through the stained-glass windows reflecting hues of gold, red and blue. Candles flickered in silent prayer for the removal of life's problems. Intoxicating fragrance from hundreds of freshly picked flowers floated over the assembly while burning incense competed for ascendancy to create a more somber mood.

It was time for the boys' weekly confession for the sins they had committed since the previous week. Constant beatings were trivial compared to the embarrassment and confusion created by confession. Three hundred boys in school uniforms had, as usual, been marched from their classrooms down the winding staircase and into the church. Jesuits carefully guarded all escape routes. Several of those students would have a strong impact on Ireland's political, legal, and cultural life, some would die young from suicide, and others would emigrate never to be heard from again.

Confession was a requirement to receive the sacrament of Holy Communion. One must not have any sins while receiving the body and blood of their Lord Jesus Christ. Murphy and the eighteen boys in his class nervously waited their turn to enter the wooden box where the priest would want to hear every lurid detail.

Murphy was always embarrassed about his sinning

that had become progressively worse. Despite so many confessions, he remained squeamish revealing details of his sins to the man in darkness who, inches from his face, usually recognized him. He was regularly glared at by the priests in the school hallways causing further discomfort.

The long line of sinners always thinned out too quickly. There were five confessional boxes with the name of the priest showing in front. Each had a reputation for severity or understanding when discussing various sins. Some went crazy if impure thoughts were revealed while others were revolted by disrespect to mothers or sisters. Once he'd got Fr. O'Carroll who was hard of hearing. "You did it HOW MANY TIMES? SPEAK UP BOY!" Murphy was mortified coming out of the box while the lads leered at him.

Fr. Durnan was the scariest. He taught them Latin and intense fear. Recently returned from Australia, wild rumors swirled around his departure from that distant land.

The type of sins determined which priest to seek out. Since Murphy's were mainly self-abuse, he usually sat outside Fr. O'Brien's box. Only one boy, Willis Welch, remained to go before Murphy would enter. "I'm done for," Willis whispered. "Why" "Was out sick for two weeks. In bed, most of the time."

The door of the confessional opened and a red-faced Mash Mahoney tumbled out. He was a goody two shoes, so what had disturbed him? Willis then went into the firing line, so Murphy sat alone nervously fidgeting. Apart from the usual, he had unsuccessfully tried to assault his sister with a heavy frying pan. But it had been in self-defense as she had been savagely beating him.

Eventually Willis came out looking decidedly uncomfortable. Murphy went in and closed the confession box door. Fr. O'Brien was listening to an old lady on the other side ramble on about her inconsequential sins. Murphy's knees began to hurt after kneeling for ten minutes. Finally, the grill swung open. In the darkness, Murphy vaguely saw a shadowy figure sitting with his elbows crossed over his chest. The purple door curtain briefly swayed and with horror Murphy recognized Fr. Durnan. Jesus Christ, what had happened to Fr. O'Brien?

"What did you say Murphy?" The priest's voice had a sharp edge.

"I was praying Father." Then quickly "Bless me father for I have sinned. It's been a week since my last confession."

Fr. Durnan glared, scratched his nose, while impatiently waiting for Murphy to continue. "Get on with it."

"I told lies Father. And I swore."

"What type of foul Anglo Saxon terminology did you use?"

"I used the F Word Father."

"How often?

"About twenty or thirty times, Father. And I took the name of our Lord in vain. And called my sister a bitch twice. And tried to hit her with a frying pan."

An exasperated Fr. Durnan sighed before commenting to nobody in particular about the lack of basic respect in this uncivilized society. Despite his subservience, Murphy had no intention of letting that one slip by. "Father you've no idea what she's like. She attacks me for no reason and I'm never allowed to hit her back because she's a girl. And she's always playing up to my dad and gets away with everything."

"Is she older than you?"

"Years older, Father."

"Respect her always and other women as well. One day you'll have a family of your own and a woman will be the mother of your children."

Murphy was confused how that had anything to do with his sister's barbaric behavior. Fr. Durnan might be a well-travelled man but was clearly clueless as to the strange ways of the female species.

"Continue. What other sins did you commit?"

Murphy's body tightened. "I had impure thoughts and actions Father."

"What boy? Stop muttering. Articulate correctly. God can hear you but I can't."

Murphy slightly raised his voice and was rewarded by a withering look from God's representative on earth.

"And how often did these actions take place?"

"Sixteen or maybe twenty times Father," whispered Murphy, his stomach knotted tightly. He didn't have a clue as to the accurate number. He always gave up counting once he'd reached double numbers.

Fr. Durnan's body swiveled around. His face was at the grill and inches from Murphy's who now had sweat dripping from his brow.

"What's wrong with you boy? It's only been a week since your last confession!"

An uncomfortable silence followed while Murphy nervously waited. "Were you alone at the time or were you with another boy, or girl or animal?"

"Father, what would I be doing with an animal?"

"Ah, I forgot, a city boy unaccustomed to rural appetites. Were you alone and if so, describe your impure thoughts."

"Alone, Father. Thinking about different things. One was with a woman I know.

"What were you doing with her?" Asked with ice in every word.

Murphy thought back to the previous night when in bed furiously jerking as his head buried itself between Biddy Ryan's bountiful breasts, a place where he'd happily suffocate to death. Suddenly he began to feel arousal and became ashamed of himself.

"I was touching her, Father, and she was touching my

privates."

Murphy failed to disclose Biddy also clawed at his back, breaking the skin when screaming in ecstasy and calling him "A fierce fuckin man altogether."

More uncomfortable silence while Fr. Durnan considered the degree of severity of Murphy's sins and the appropriate punishment. There was movement as he raised his arm to his mouth. When he turned back to Murphy a strong whiskey smell reminded Murphy of his father.

"Yes," mumbled Fr. Durnan.

Having no idea what was expected from him Murphy simply responded "Yes, Father"

A calmer Fr. Durnan now. "Listen to me child, if you don't stop that filthy behavior it will lead to great problems later in life. Believe me you'll end up in trouble you now know nothing about. Best solve your problem or you'll be paying for it later, here and into eternity. Remember that."

How to solve his problem perplexed Murphy but he knew better than to ask how it might be achieved. The confessional box was the only place he ever told anybody about his filthy behavior. He also wanted to ask Fr. Durnan what was the point of coming back to confession every week to confess the same sins only to return the following week to confess and repent again and be forgiven by God. It made no sense at all. But wisely he remained silent.

"Your penance is ten Our Fathers, ten Hail Mary's, ten Glory Be's, and pray for my intentions."

Murphy decided not to ask what those intentions were. Fr. Durnan blessed Murphy while reciting words in Latin thereby absolving the boy from all his sins. Relief joyfully flowed through Murphy. His soul was temporarily cleansed from all impurities.

"Thank you, Father."

Making the sign of the cross, Murphy rose and left the confessional. He felt lightheaded. Confession wasn't that bad. After doing his penance, there was a spring in his step as he walked with head bowed to receive Holy Communion.

Michael Cassidy

Chapter Eleven

FIRST DANCE

"Well now, look at himself. Very handsome, yes, very nice INDEED!" His mother's voice reached hi/m from behind a cloud of cigarette smoke. Murphy's father was in his comfortable leather seat, right hand resting on his face as he turned away from the fire to look at his youngest child. Murphy's pampered sister, Grainne. sat by her father's legs looking like the puppy dog she was, while his brother, Liam, silently sipped his tea, observing everything.

The grandfather clock in the hall chimed seven-thirty. He couldn't delay any longer. The hop started at eight.

"Good luck. You'll need it," laughed the wicked witch of the north in a high pitched derisive tone.

"Never mind her, son. You'll have a grand time altogether." A break in the clouds showed his mother glaring icily at his sister. Served her right.

Murphy was growing up fast, but not fast enough. Now fifteen, he'd been attending the Jesuit school for nine years. The Jesuits were acknowledged as excellent educators but all Murphy learned was through fear, with daily punishments and beatings being the norm rather than the exception. One day a few months before, a knock came to the classroom door. Fr. Durnan warned that anyone who looked when it opened would be punished; all eyes must be focused on the blackboard. Being the way he was Murphy couldn't resist looking, so a delighted Fr. Durnan immediately handed him a docket to be punished with six of the best from the Prefect of Studies.

"Ah you yet again, Murphy. What have you done THIS time?" Murphy timidly handed over the docket. "Mmmm so which pandy-bat should I use on you? You make a suggestion." Murphy looked up at the variety of leather straps swaying gently in the open window breeze. "How about that one, Father?" pointing to one he knew to be somewhat less painful than the others. "I think not. Let's use this one." Fr. Trodden took an extra thick, long one, chuckling at some private joke as he did so. Unwisely Murphy pulled back as the fourth strike came swishing down from above Fr. Trodden's head. That resulted in him getting eight instead of six. The one he'd pulled back from, that completely numbed the top of his hand, did not count. As always, after the beating, he had to say, "Thank you, Father."

Fortunately, he was academically bright and a very good athlete and rugby player. That somewhat helped to distract punishments he might otherwise have incurred. He lived for rugby and thrived on the joy it gave him. He played for the school teams where other players were two years older than him and this delighted his father who attended every match. After winning games he'd be in his local pub, rest a hand on his son›s shoulder, and boast to the other men about his boy's latest winning play. Murphy, flushed with the pride of it, would sit quietly soaking up his father's approval while drinking Lucozade and eating Taytos.

Now, in a few moments, he'd be on his way out the door to his first dance. He caught a quick glance at himself in the mirror and liked what he saw. His new suit, together with matching shirt and tie, looked good and so did he. Periwinkle shoes finished off the job. He hummed Ricky Nelson's latest hit song, "Traveling Man" as he splashed his father's Old Spice aftershave liberally over his disappointingly whiskerless face.

"You'll have a grand ole time," his mother said encouragingly, but with what he thought was a tremor in her voice. A closer look showed that she was crying a little. Her baby boy was growing up and becoming independent. Soon she'd no longer be needed.

"I will," I agreed.

"Be home by ten o clock."

The whole family was standing on the porch waving enthusiastically as he began his solitary walk out the gate then up the Avenue. Jesus, thought Murphy, you'd swear he was leaving for America never to be seen again.

The further away he got from home the more a feeling of elation settled on him. After years of waiting, of watching his brother and sister head off to hops, he was finally old enough to attend them and, maybe this time, even shift a girl if he could figure out the knack. He'd regularly practiced kissing the bathroom mirror to try and get the hang of it but always felt ridiculous when he saw his squished face looking back at himself.

He felt considerably less comfortable as he came closer to the dance hall at his school. Butterflies began to hop around inside his stomach. He seriously considered turning back and going home. The dance was a stupid idea anyway. He was about to turn around when who did he see but Rashers O'Brien.

"How's it going? Are ye here for the hop?" Rashers sounded like there was a clothes peg on his nose.

"Yep," Murphy responded. "And yourself?"

"Yeah, thought I'd check it out."

"Been before?" asked very casually.

"Yeah, once," buzzed Rashers through his nostrils.

Across the road people were walking up to the entrance of his school and paying their ten shillings' fee. As the door swung open Murphy heard the band doing a Brendan Boyer song:

"Hey hey, here's a dance you should KNOW,
Oh baby, when the lights are down LOW

If you don't know it then you're out of LUCK
Take you baby's hand, twist her all AROUND
Wiggle like a snake, wobble like a DUCK
YEAH, that's how you do, do the HUCKLEBUCK."

"And?" I asked.

Rashers looked blankly at him.

"What was it like?" Murphy persisted.

"Ah, OK, you know."

"If I did I wouldn't ask you. So, what was it like?"

"Ah, dancing and stuff like that."

Idiot. By then Murphy was ready to kick the bejesus out of Rashers but was prevented from doing so since they were almost there. Somehow walking alongside his schoolmate had restored his sense of well-being. Rashers was a nice person; his regular golf partner, but it was safe to say that he would never be convicted of being a ladies' man. He had the mournful look of a mortician and was dressed like he was going to a funeral, black everything. He was very tall, beyond skinny, and awkward, always about to trip over himself. He wore thick glasses balanced on a long nose with nostrils that seemed to simultaneously move in several directions like a bloodhound sniffing the scent. Beneath the flailing nostrils was a suggestion of a moustache that failed to hide his crooked teeth. His father was a dentist but obviously not a good one. And the way Rashers talked! Bloody hell! If he could survive a hop with all his deficiencies and come back for more then, Murphy thought, he'd undoubtedly have no problem.

Having lined up, they paid their ten shillings and entered. Show time! The band was now playing a waltz called, "Il Silensio." A little baldheaded man blew into a trumpet almost as big as himself while the five other members of the band strummed guitars and hummed along. The girls packed tightly together on one side of the hall with the boys on the opposite side seemed to Murphy like warring tribes suspiciously keeping a hard eye on earth other. Couples were dancing but, of course, not too closely as that might result in the boys having impure thoughts. There were red, yellow, and blue balloons everywhere, and in the right-hand corner a mineral water stand. Murphy noticed they also sold ice cream and Taytos. A few lads walked over with girls and bought them drinks. They then stood awkwardly feigning indifference, some talking, some not, but almost all looking uncomfortable as they gazed blankly into space.

Rashers and Murphy walked over to get a mineral. They wouldn't have so many people gawking at them if they at least appeared to be doing something. The hall was almost full with boys and girls whose average age was sixteen. The inevitable priests dressed in their black outfits constantly circled the hall with mournful faces, hands clasped tightly behind their backs, watching hawk-like for any inappropriate behavior. Murphy had no doubt their flabby arses would fall off if even a hint of a smile began to appear on their miserable faces.

An authoritative voice bellowed into the microphone. It was cherubic Cornelius Hannagan, a family friend and prominent member of society who, at a future date, would subsequently molest Murphy. "Great job! Il Silensio. Lovely, let's hear it for the lads!"

Everyone hooted, hollered, and clapped loudly.

"Now ladies and gentlemen. The next dance is a ladies' choice," Cornelius, who would never dance with any lady, enthusiastically announced.

Holy mother of Jesus, nobody had told Murphy about that. Fortunately, he was still close to the door so could do a runner if necessary. What if no girl asked him to dance and he was left stuck here with Rashers the gawky Beanstalk? Most of the boys suddenly found the need to become involved in animated discussions with other boys while the girls cautiously eyed them up. "Come on now girls. Ladies choice," roared Cornelius noting no girl had yet asked anyone to dance. Murphy was mesmerized as he watched them fan out, carefully examining their prey before pouncing. The line he was in began to thin. Rashers, not surprisingly, was still standing beside him.

"Will ye dance?" A lovely girl, perhaps fourteen or fifteen, possessing exceptional wisdom, had chosen Murphy from the unruly mob. She had fair hair that seemed to bounce around her head even as she stood before him, clear blue eyes, and a confident smile. Dressed in a yellow and white striped dress that went down below her knees, her smile welcomed him into her world. She even had all her teeth which were amazingly white. Mary was her name. Even when she couldn't hear Murphy because of the noise of the band, she still smiled and laughed at all his garbled comments. Janie Mac, this was a cinch, realized Murphy while wildly shaking his hips and moving his feet from side to side at a furious pace, just the way he'd practiced so many times in the privacy of his bedroom. Elvis watch out!

The band was playing another Chubby Checker song.

"Come on Baby let's do the Twist,

Like we did last summer,

Let's do the Twist, Twisting time is here."

Mary and Murphy twisted away with the fierce intensity of youth and as they did, he still managed to gasp out plenty of questions. He'd overheard one of the older lads at school last week who was great with the women say that if you asked them loads of questions they'd think you were a good talker even though they were the ones doing all the talking. Murphy didn't really understand why that worked but it was certainly worth a try. Mary went to Laurel Hill. He realized her dad and his were in Rotary together and they had met at an international Rotary convention in Killarney some years before when they were young. But she'd grown up a lot since then, and seemed to have a delightful new shape lurking beneath that dress. He wondered if he should offer to buy her a Fanta or Coke. What was expected of him? Damn, he should have asked brother John or even his sister what the etiquette was.

The set ended and couples stood deciding if they wanted to stay for another dance or not. It only took a few seconds but these were vital moments especially after a Ladies Choice when it was clear the girl liked the boy. He watched as some couples remained on the floor, a few of them brazenly holding hands. Others walked over for a mineral, ice cream or Taytos. But most, like Murphy, were clueless novices who simply said, "Thanks," then hastened a retreat back to the sanctuary of the boys' section of the hall.

The next set was about to begin. Ear splitting noise preceded Murphy being roughly pushed aside and almost knocked into next week by the herd of bulls who thundered across the hall to where the girls stood waiting with welcoming smiles. Years later Murphy would run with the bulls in Pamplona. That experience would be mild compared to the dance madness.

But he was quickly learning the game. You spotted a girl, then watched for when the music was about to begin because you didn't want to be out in the open all by yourself when it started. On the other hand, the danger of waiting too long opened the possibility the girl that interested you could already be snapped up. It obviously required precise timing and tactical positioning. He sat that dance out but before the next one began, he knew who he wanted and watched carefully as she walked back toward the girls' side. She was dark with Black Irish looks and brown, fluttering eyes that seemed to flash hello as she passed by. But was it merely his wishful thinking? Only one way to find out. Across from no man's land she was laughing with her hand over her mouth and talking to her friend who was giggling. They seemed to be looking over at Murphy. He wondered if they laughing at him. But if so, why? He waved and they waved back. Looking good. But you could never be too sure. He'd heard frightening stories about lads asking a girl to dance only for the girl refusing to separate from her friends. The long walk back to safety would be humiliating. Butterflies had returned to his stomach as he prepared to make his assault.

He was already half way across the room and ahead of everyone else when the music began. Oh shit! It was a slow one. Too late to stop. "Would you like to dance?' A horrifying pause, then she smiled and offered her hand. He quickly marched her out onto the dance floor before she could change her mind and joined the procession that, clockwise, was slowly circling the hall. He wished it was a fast dance since he'd never practiced the waltz and was painfully conscious of where he was putting his feet. Hopefully, he wouldn't cripple her for life. Her hair smelled of strawberries. He wondered about telling her but was afraid it would sound ridiculous. Her name was Mareid and she went to school at Presentation. That was good because he'd heard from the older lads that girls from Presentation were much faster than Laurel Hill girls. Most of them allowed you to kiss them on a first date. He couldn't resist a quick peek down the top of Mareid's dress.

"What are ye staring at?" she asked, knowing full well.

Murphy panicked. "God, you're bloody well lovely," was all he could think of to say. And it worked! Mareid glowed with delight!

"You're a fast one, aren't you," she responded while moving closer to him. He felt himself getting hard below and was horrified she'd notice. Fortunately, the song soon ended.

Emboldened by her response, and learning from his previous mistake, he quickly asked her to stay for another dance and she seemed delighted at the suggestion. They danced away with Murphy swiveling his hips, flailing his arms madly into the air while throwing his entire body into what probably resembled an epileptic fit, but he didn't give a damn. He was feeling great! They shouted questions and observations into each other's ears as Cornelius smiled heartily on the stage while carefully scanning the dancers.

The set ended. Silence as Mareid looked up at him waiting for him to take the lead. But if he asked her for another dance would that mean he was supposed to stay with her for the rest of the evening? Was he supposed to ask if he could have her home number or would that be too forward? This girl stuff was exhausting! A constantly changing scenario with no manual on what to do. After several uncomfortable moments of silence, he panicked again, said "Thanks" then walked away leaving her looking at his back. She paused as if about to say something, shrugged her shoulders, then quickly walked back to the girls' side. Cursing his stupidity, he chastised himself for failing to offer her a lemonade. Damn it to hell anyway.

Rashers was standing in the same spot where he'd left him. He hadn't danced even once. No ladies' choice for him. "Well, you're doing grand," he whistled between the gurgles coming from the bottom of a Fanta bottle. His face was red from the exertion of sucking on the straw.

"Ah well, you know," Murphy replied with an expansive wave. An old hand by now, a master at the art. He danced seven more times that evening, getting asked up on both other ladies' choices.

The journey home bore no resemblance to the path he'd taken to the dance. He whistled, full of the joys of life as he reflected on the sounds, scents, and sights of the evening. The girls' various perfumes had him intoxicated; all different, all dangerously enticing. The strange feelings he'd felt especially when dancing close; a mixture of exhilaration and confusion. Clearly, he had much to learn about girls and their strange ways but he'd made a solid start. No goddammit, he'd made a wonderful start! "I did it!" he shouted to no one as he began his triumphant walk down the hill towards home.

Since it was ten thirty-five, he hoped he wouldn't be in trouble. Usually he went in by the side door, but tonight he'd been given a key to the front because of the occasion that was in it. The door opened before he had the key in the lock.

"Well?" several voices blurted at once. The family had been awaiting his return.

"Well what?" he responded indifferently as if they were asking for an inconsequential weather report. He strode victoriously into the living room. The fire was roaring and hot, fresh tea called to him from the waiting teapot. He rubbed his hands vigorously before the flames, keeping his overcoat on while seemingly lost in thought and outwardly indifferent to their urgent pleadings.

"Ah come on, did anyone agree to dance with you?" asked Grainne hoping the answer would be no.

"Actually, they were fighting over me for the Ladies choices. It was grand. And I danced nearly every dance." he smugly responded.

Relieved, his mother clapped her hands in delight, her cheeks glowing. "Oh, you have it all. You can do everything, near the top of your class at school, captain of the rugby team, on the athletics team, and now this!"

His father, sitting in his seat, hands in pockets, watched the scene unfold with a sparkle in his eye and thoroughly enjoying the spectacle. Liam generously congratulated him, while Grainne coldly observed while trying to determine the extent of his lies.

More animated chatting followed, then it was well past time for bed. Murphy brushed his teeth, got into his pajamas, and crawled under the covers. He replayed every aspect of the night; his lonely journey to the hop, handing over ten bob at the door, feeling like an untrained gladiator entering the Coliseum, the heat, the popping balloons, the girl's hand in his, the occasional feel of a brassiere strap under a dress, the band blasting out the beat as his body contorted along with two hundred other innocent, Irish boys and girls sweating it out on the floor, the disappointment of it being over so quickly, then the triumphant arrival home.

He laughed at himself for having been unnecessarily nervous; there was nothing to fear. Easy, shmeezy. His mother was right. He did have it all!

Chapter Twelve

PUNISHMENT

Biddy McGrath's bountiful breasts wobbled before his eager mouth like pears bopping in a Halloween bowl. A stinging blow to his face created another reality. Giant hand ready to strike again, Father Bull O'Callaghan SJ towered like a victorious prizefighter as Murphy swallowed blood.

"Father?"

"The answer Master Murphy, or did Goethe labor to see his genius wasted on imbeciles like you?"

Murphy struggled to get up while frantically trying to remember something, anything.

"Sorry, Father. I must have become distracted."

Bull O'Callaghan took it as a personal insult if his four pupils disrespected his favorite poet's work. Hissing and puffing, he threw his text book at another student who unsuccessfully dodged the book hitting his face. Murphy naively hoped he was safe. But nobody was ever safe in those classrooms. Fear of fear, of being called on and being revealed as incompetent, ugly, and an idiot was always lurking, ready to strike.

"Well," decided the Bull turning back to Murphy. "Perhaps six of the best will help focus your attention. But somehow, I doubt it."

Murphy felt immense relief. Being on the receiving end of the Bull's anger was unpleasant. He was as tall as wide. His angry purple face always looked as if it was about to explode. Thick, dark glasses, suggesting no eyes, added to his evil presence. Getting away with punishment from the

Prefect of Studies was almost fun compared to facing the Bull's wrath.

"Now Master Murphy, recite this wonderful poem. I dare you to disrespect it by using dreadful pronunciation."

"Am brunen for dem taura

Da stedt ein lindenbaum

Ich shit in zeina rinde."

He knew what was coming when the Bull first froze in horror then threw himself at the stupid, stuttering boy cowering underneath him. Smells of whiskey, tobacco and disgust mixed with primal violence poured like fresh lava from the Bull. Trembling, his eyes ablaze with fury, he held the boy dangling in mid-air. Murphy's nervous reaction was to start giggling.

"Ah, you find this amusing, Master Murphy!"

He dropped Murphy like a sack of unwanted spuds then slowly raised an open hand covered in nicotine, chalk and sweat. Swinging hard that hand covered Murphy's face when it landed. Being captain of the Bull's rugby team clearly was no advantage.

"Life is weary."

Then he hit the other side of Murphy's face.

Bang.

"Life is hard."

Back now to the other side to ensure equity in the punishment

"And the goal"

Blood now flowed from the nostrils. Confusion. Brief loss of consciousness.

"Is not the grave!"

This time even harder to safely make his point.

Although humiliated and in pain, Murphy felt great anger rise inside him. He quietly swore when fully grown he'd search for the Bull and cruelly subject him to worse punishment.

"Now get out, clean yourself up and go down to the Prefect of Studies."

The other boys, feeling sorry for Murphy, fidgeted nervously wondering who would be next.

His classroom was on the fourth floor. Along the walls bored looking stuffed birds and an assortment of foxes hung. Photos of Crescent boys who had gone on to make their mark in the world covered the entire third floor.

Winding his way down the staircase, the sound of a punishment rang in his ears. Quietly he approached the Prefect of Studies office. A child was crying and asking Fr. Trodyn to stop as his hand was more firmly grasped. He bawled as the final belts rained down. Had better get used to it, Murphy thought, then realized he needed to clean up otherwise face more interrogation about what he had done to deserve the punishment. That'd make more trouble. Better not to mention it at home either because that would create another beating for causing trouble at school. Ten minutes later, a calmer and more presentable Murphy presented himself.

Fr. Trodyn wheezed as he carried out his duty. His nicotine fingers selected an appropriate leather strap. Apart from the clash of leather on flesh, the only sound came from an old clock with a bird who sang a gentle lullaby. "Six for insubordination. Hmmm"

An undefinable inner anger replaced the physical pain. Outside it was raining. Shadows darkened the schoolyard. Herds of elephants floated in the afternoon sky. Shouts from teenage boys playing soccer in the yard below. They worked for the Jesuits. Only recently, a brilliant academic and athlete, Brendan Reagan, who had been selected to play soccer for Ireland, was ordered not to play, but did. He was expelled for insubordination. Jesuit boys do not play working class sports.

Punishment completed, he began to walk out of the office.

"Haven't you forgotten something Murphy?"

Murphy paused a moment, then, "Thank you, Father".

Chapter Thirteen

DANGERS OF THE FLESH

As Head of Morality, Father Morrissey vehemently warned about the evils of lust and the danger of women in general. He warned them about taking pleasure from their own or other people's bodies. It began relatively innocently as a venial sin but would inevitably escalate to mortal, then a one-way ticket to hell. The result would be eternal damnation for a few fleeting moments of illicit pleasure. Proving the validity of his thesis, Father Morrissey disappeared early one morning with a young country girl. He subsequently sired two children with her.

Impure thoughts or actions were the central point of all morality. The ten commandments in Ireland had been reduced to one. Burning in hell for eternity seemed an acceptable, if somewhat extreme, trade-off for the young boys. One way to overcome the dilemma was to attend eight First Friday masses in a row, then receive Holy Communion. That guaranteed the sinner automatic entry into heaven regardless of the type or severity of sins committed. Unfortunately, Murphy knew of only two boys who had ever managed to do it. The rest of them would inevitably fry in hell with the bad women on the docks, the black babies in Africa who had not been baptized, and the millions of misfortunate Protestants and Jews who had never been baptized in the Catholic church.

Murphy had never really kissed a girl. Two years before he'd shifted Nuala Griffin in the shed but it was awful. Taller than he, Nuala dribbled while also smelling of burnt grease, rashers, and onions. He'd also tried to shift Nina

Gallagher in her dining room but she was having none of it and threatened to tell his mother. Girls were such tattletales.

Having no other outlet for his newly found passion, Murphy lay in his bed thinking of the naked girls he'd seen in his father's carefully hidden Playboy magazine. Weather was hot and so was he. A summer breeze rose from the Shannon river and blew through the ancient pine trees creating a comforting swishing sound. He heard Rory, who had taken over Jamsie's duties with the nuns, shouting to his sheep dog. A cooling breeze floated in the window making the room cooler.

It was early June of his sixteenth year. The house was quiet apart from the radio playing Bobby Darin's new hit song "Multiplication," It would soon be banned from broadcast by the Catholic church because of its suggestive lyrics.

Murphy pressed himself against his bed and felt the heat rising. His thoughts drifted to Mary, a girl from the Mount girls' school who was mad for it and, importantly, seemed to like him. She wanted to meet him at Punch's Cross that very evening.

When the time drew close he cleaned himself, liberally splashed on his father's Old Spice aftershave, then nonchalantly wandered up the Avenue. Soon the promised land was smiling invitingly at him. Mary reached out to greet him by eagerly taking him into her arms while also landing a wet one. Then she was nibbling on his ear focusing mainly on his earlobe. What the hell was she doing. And why? Wondered a confused Murphy hoping the grease in his ear would not make her sick. She then moved on to his neck happily nibbling as she travelled. Please don't leave me with marks thought Murphy knowing, if noticed, he'd face an embarrassing interrogation at home.

Taking a break from devouring him, Mary pulled

Murphy deeper into the shadows while telling him how happy she was they were together. He was also happy and now very hard which seemed to please rather than disgust a smiling Mary who pushed up against him.

"Will you have a bag of Taytos or a Lucozade or what?"

"I've got all that stuff at home. No one's there."

Mary's warm smile reached out to him as did her right hand. She took his and placed it inside her now opened school blouse. An astonished Murphy couldn't believe his luck!

Being a girl who did not stand on ceremony, once home, Mary immediately took him upstairs to her bedroom, dragged him onto the bed and started fiercely kissing him. Murphy felt he'd been swallowed by a vacuum cleaner.

Mary got off the bed, walked towards the mirror then turned about and began to slowly unbutton her blouse. Then she turned her back for Murphy to unhook her bra. His trembling hands could not open the clasps. Laughing, Mary did it herself then, cupping her quarter moon breasts, offered herself to Murphy who was delighted to oblige. Unfortunately, just as they were really getting into it, the glare of headlights swept across the room. Mary's parents had unexpectedly come home. A frustrated Mary helped a terrified Murphy struggle into his clothes before he unhesitatingly jumped out the second story bedroom window. His fall was eased by landing deep into soil that for months had nurtured an assortment of just ripened, but now destroyed, vegetables.

That Friday, he attended weekly confession and proudly announced his adventures to an unenthusiastic Fr. O'Brien who warned him this loose woman was absolutely an occasion of sin and should be avoided always. "Your mortal soul is in great danger!" he warned a delighted Murphy before giving him a heavy penance.

Being weak willed, Murphy happily endangered his

soul in exchange for many blissful experiences with Mary. Just to be safe, he was determined to do eight First Friday masses and holy communion. But he never did.

Chapter Fourteen

UNKNOWABLE ANGEL

Murphy knew the cockerel would never crow three times because he'd betrayed his redeemer. When he ate the body, and drank the blood of his Lord Jesus Christ, no earthly language could adequately describe the intensity of his feelings. Sometimes an overflowing volcano of joy exploded inside him; other times tears of sadness and shame flowed when he looked up at the statues and saw Jesus with a haunted expression of loneliness while gruesomely nailed to the cross, blood freely dripping from outstretched arms and feet. "Father why hast thou forsaken me?" Christ asked in confusion while looking up to heaven for the existence of a father who had abandoned Him.

Each time before receiving the sacrament of Holy Communion, Murphy solemnly bowed his head and recited what had been beaten into him. "Lord, I am not worthy to receive You. Say but the word and my soul shall be healed."

Occasionally he'd think back to the nuns as they prepared the then six-year-olds for first communion. It had been an extremely serious business. "Now boys and girls, close your eyes, firmly stick out your tongue, slowly, carefully close your mouth then swallow. You don't want Jesus falling onto a dirty floor. No licking, playing with the tongue, or putting it into the side of your mouth." The children were sternly warned that should they commit that offense it would count as a mortal sin and would have to be reported to the priest when confessing their venial sins.

Before the big day, his sister, Grainne, insisted on

endless practice sessions. She'd preen in smug delight as she took on the role of priest by delicately placing pieces of bread onto his tongue. Then she'd roar mercilessly if she decided he wasn't doing it right or being sufficiently solemn. Terrified by the lash of her tongue, he was convinced he'd disgrace the whole family on first communion day by panicking, then getting into convulsions and spitting Jesus out of his mouth. He suffered several sleepless nights punctuated by horrifying images of the Bishop roaring condemnation at him in Latin, while also excommunicating him. This was all accompanied by approving howls of an equally outraged congregation led by his disappointed parents who chased him from the church and banished him from civilized society. But apart from crying a few times during the ceremony, he behaved correctly and was reasonably optimistic his mother would not beat him that day for his misbehavior.

Now in his teens, although he went to mass and benediction each week at his Jesuit school, he also liked to occasionally attend morning mass at the Redemptorist Church located near his home. It was an austere building that retained a semblance of restrained elegance. It also boasted about having the largest Arch Confraternity in the world.

It was there that it happened early one November morning. God's white robed representative on earth had turned his back around to face the small congregation, put his left hand into a golden chalice then marched to the front of the altar. With precious Latin words, almost two thousand years old, he had taken what had, until moments before, been an insignificant piece of bread and magically transformed it into God's body. The priest muttered more words and the inexpensive red wine sitting in another chalice mysteriously became the blood of Jesus.

Taking the host into his mouth, with hands clasped and head bowed, Murphy returned to his seat, knelt, and prayed with the unrestrained joy of the believer. God sat patiently on his tongue ready to first slide down his throat, then deep through his insides, before eventually entering his soul. Murphy had always worried about what happened to God after he'd digested Him. What happened when Murphy needed to poop? That seemed disgusting so he assumed that the Holy Ghost scooped Him up and flew Him away in time before He suffered the indignity of being flushed down into the smelly sewers, then flowing into the filthy, polluted Shannon River.

He'd just finished praying when he sensed her presence. A glorious whiff of elegant perfume and luxurious soap drifted on the air, contrasting mightily with the harshness of incense. The Angel floated by dressed in a crisply starched Laurel Hill school uniform. He became transfixed, confused then transformed into a babbling idiot state and started giggling uncontrollably. Some old wans glared angrily at him from behind their black shawlies.

The Angel went up to receive Holy Communion. He'd never seen such beauty. She put Grace Kelly to shame! He estimated her to be approximately two years older and a foot taller than himself. When she walked back and passed by, his giggling had fortunately stopped and been replaced by a complete paralysis of his body combined with a frightening shortage of breath. Ten eternal minutes later the mass mercifully ended and the church emptied. He was finally able to move his limbs, and staggered out of the now empty church.

Desperately needing to see her again, he got up every morning at an ungodly hour and happily endured shivering up the hill against the blinding rain and bitter cold so he could attend the same mass. One long week later he was rewarded when she majestically entered the church. He savored every milli-second of her regal procession as she delicately floated over the marble floor before genuflecting then kneeling in the pew. He caught a brief glimpse of her white slip and shamefully experienced an impure thought which he quickly exorcized from his previously unsoiled mind.

At communion time, he rudely forced himself in front of two indignant old ladies so that he was standing directly behind his Angel. By moving his head closer he could better smell her chestnut brown hair. Momentarily deranged, he moved very close so he was almost touching her neck. His Angel must have sensed the enthusiastic breathing on her because she turned around and gave him a withering look. Panicking he responded with what he hoped was a confident, reassuring smile but which his Angel seemed to interpret as a disgusting, lecherous leer. She didn't scream, but hissed "GO AWAY!" from the thick, full, blood red lips of her beautifully formed mouth. Horrified, Murphy hastily backed away and in the process banged into the already offended old ladies, knocking both onto the ground in the process. All eyes were glaring at him including his Angel and a thoroughly annoyed priest. Murphy wanted to die. "Please God, take me now!"

Helping the helped the angry ladies off the floor, he then hastily retreated. He didn't dare go back for communion.

The Angel knelt at the altar and he noticed her brown stockings modestly covering the most beautiful long legs he had ever seen. Intently, he watched her delicate mouth open like a bird in the nest waiting impatiently to be fed. The knuckles of his Angel's hands were white from holding them clasped tightly in prayer. He sat transfixed as her tongue darted forward to take the holy sacrament into her eagerly waiting open mouth.

After Mass, she paused to pull her overcoat tightly around her before braving the elements. Murphy watched from a safe distance and noticed her shiver. To make up for his embarrassing blunder he considered running to her, bravely taking off his coat, and insisting she put it over her shoulders for warmth. She would admire his manliness and instantly forgive him, then be charmed by his eloquence and brilliant wit. Fortunately, he decided not to compound his stupidity and realized he could think of nothing to say and would be too shy even if he had a perfectly prepared script. So instead he kept a discreet distance.

Outside it was black and cold but the sleet had temporarily stopped. She turned left onto O'Connell Street. He waited momentarily before walking to the corner, then peeked. An old biddy passing by gave him a queer look. He didn't care. His Angel was walking down the hill. He hoped she wouldn't walk too far; he had to be home soon for breakfast. His mother would be wondering where he was. The Angel stopped at the bottom of the hill just before the corner at Frawley's chemist shop, opened the gate and walked into a large, red brick house. So, that was where she lived!

He went to many earlier morning masses just to catch a glimpse of her. His mother was surprised but very pleased by his increased devotion to God and wondered if he had a vocation for the priesthood.

Countless times as he lay in bed, or was daydreaming at school, he relived, with his Angel, some of the experiences he'd read of in his mother's magazines; the ones he wasn't supposed to read and which his father considered unmitigated rubbish. It was the special sparkle they put in his mother's eyes for a time after reading them that had first got Murphy interested. And so, in his fertile imagination his Angel and he wandered worry free through summer meadows rich with multicolored flowers that swayed and danced in celebration of their love. Bees sucked pollen in the shimmering afternoon glow as, much to her delight, he sophisticatedly placed kisses on his Angel's face.

They were oblivious to the distractions of an outside world where people rushed about frantically chasing illusions. No problems could penetrate the protective veil created by the power of their spectacular love. Unperturbed, they ate French cheese and freshly baked baguettes, sipped from a bottle of Matheus Rose wine his mother had kept hidden, and talked lazily about their future together. Alone in the world those fields bordered their oneness. Nothing could harm them.

With her head resting comfortably on his lap he effortlessly recited poems by Yeats, Wordsworth, Byron, and love sonnets from Shakespeare, while her worshipping eyes looked up at him with stunned admiration wondering how he could possibly know so much about life and art. Later, he made chains of yellow and white daisies, taken fresh from the soil, and placed them in her waist long hair while she unashamedly, and quite understandably, proclaimed her love for him. She being two years older meant nothing to her. Age was simply an irrelevant number. His raw intelligence and overall sophistication more than compensated for any age difference. She recognized him as a man amongst boys. To hell with what other people said about them! They were in love. Nothing else mattered.

Although he saw her at several other early morning masses, it took him two months before he summoned the courage to finally approach her. The night before he planned to throw his hat into the ring for her affections he spent ages practicing a speech in front of the bathroom mirror. He desperately searched for witty opening lines that would have her immediately smiling and realizing how mature, witty, and wise he was. Usually he was good at writing essays in school but nothing in his life had prepared him for this daunting task. Dejected, he finally gave up and trudged gloomily to bed.

That Thursday morning, very cold it was, he had to force himself out from under the warm bedcovers. The January wind howled as he battled his way up the Avenue against the piercing rain. Logic shouted at him to wise up and return to his cozy bed and comforting hot water bottle.

But for a glimpse of his Angel he'd climb Mount Everest blindfolded, with two broken legs, arms tied behind his back and not a Sherpa in sight.

He thought gently about her in a futile effort to distract himself from the inclement weather. Darkness didn't help his mood. Streetlights wouldn't be turned on for another hour. Occasionally a light flickered from a house; otherwise the Avenue was blanketed in darkness. Finally, he made it to the Redemptorist Church, forced the giant doors open, and eagerly looked for her. He wished it were summertime so he could have come with a bouquet of flowers hidden in his overcoat. But that didn't matter because she wasn't there. Surely his angel would reappear? But she didn't.

After another nerve wracking month attending early morning Mass he reluctantly accepted defeat. She was gone. Despite his misery, he prayed she was safe and well wherever she might be. But he never again darkened the doors of that ugly church.

Meanwhile, impressed by his newly acquired religious fervor, his mother gleefully arranged an appointment for him to talk with Fr. McKenna, the spiritual advisor at his school, to discuss her son's vocation for the priesthood.

Chapter Fifteen

SCHOOL ENDS

The powerful aroma of incense emanating from swinging thuribles permeated the atmosphere before lazily drifting upwards in a cloudy wave taking Murphy's thoughts with it as the mass progressed. The day he'd dreamed of had finally arrived! After thirteen long years, his school days at the Crescent were finally over. It was an eternity since, as a terrified child, he'd clung to the Longfellah's comforting hand and struggled up those concrete steps, through the towering doors and into the great unknown. Now those same doors were small.

He studied the faces around him, once young boys now grown into early manhood. "Give me a child, and he's mine for life," was a Jesuit mantra. Despite being repeatedly told over the years how stupid and foolish they were, several of the boys in his class would have a profound future impact on Ireland.

Murphy experienced mixed emotions during his final hours at school. He was quietly confident about his upcoming final exams. They would determine his future. The only subject of concern was Irish. Despite having a natural aptitude for languages, he had difficulty mastering Irish. Unfortunately, due to the prevalent nationalistic fervor, if Murphy did not pass his Irish exam, despite receiving honors in all other subjects, he would fail everything. `

These impressionable children had been systematically molded into the image of what the authorities believed a Jesuit boy should be. Years of indoctrination had confirmed, in their conscious and subconscious minds, their social and intellectual superiority over the lesser classes who would always be needed to work the machinery.

Despite his anger at the system, Murphy felt strangely nostalgic after being herded into his final school mass. Father Trodyn and others who oversaw the "prison", all stood somberly, unsmiling, rigidly upright with hands behind backs.

Murphy was dealing with other confusing problems but had no idea what specifically was wrong with him or why. Nothing was ever enough. "If only" constantly swirled inside his head. Despite seeming comfortable with the world, inside he was constantly ill at ease. At age sixteen, he had earned five honors from seven subjects in the national exams. That was good he thought, but what if he had received six? When he made an exciting move during a rugby game, yes that was good, but why not another? The girl he was with was indeed lovely, but if only she had the other girls' laughter, smile, or body. His only true escape came from knocking back lots of booze and getting completely messed up. Then he entered a different world where he experienced moments of perceived clarity and freedom from fear. Those drinking sprees also provided a temporary escape from the angry God who had condemned him to burn in hell for eternity, from the priests whose day was not complete without beatings, from the unhappiness in his mother's eyes, from being indoctrinated to believe, despite his shortcomings, he was superior to other classes in society; angry because of the injustices he saw around him but was told to ignore. And so, he energetically chased, and often captured, that sense of euphoria he'd first experienced in his grandmother's house that Christmas so long ago.

The class had arranged for a formal dance the next day in Cruise's hotel. He'd invited Mareid, a lovely girl from Dublin he'd met in Kilkee that summer. She'd travelled down from Dublin, and was staying with her aunt on the Ennis road. He'd collect her around six. But first he was going with Tommy Hickey to a court hearing in Six Mile Bridge. Tommy had recently been arrested for being drunk and disorderly at a dance there. The hearing was at noon so there would be plenty of time to get back and collect Mareid.

Murphy met Tommy at South's pub where he'd obviously arrived long before. A half hour later saw them arrive at the courthouse which stood in the center of town. If the case went badly, Murphy planned to engage in a passionate defense of his friend, throwing him onto the mercy of the court, explaining Tommy was the unfortunate product of generations of indiscriminate inbreeding. One look at him would make that a convincing argument. However, it mattered not because they'd arrived a day late. Tommy paid the ten shillings fine then the lads went off to celebrate.

Tommy insisted they stop off at Shannon airport to see if any uninhibited American girls had just landed hoping to experience that uniquely American concept of "finding themselves" in Ireland. These lovelies provided a delightful alternative to the, show me the ring first, Irish virgins. Unfortunately for these American girls, they found the lads but usually lost themselves resulting in a lifetime of unsuccessful therapy. On the rare occasion they were not inclined to romance, Tommy would produce a letter from America and hand it to Murphy. The letter, written by Murphy, was allegedly from the mother of a girlfriend of his in California. She'd been killed in a motor cycle accident! That usually resulted in gushing maternal outpourings with the girl passionately holding Murphy while he genuinely wept enough tears to flood the house. But if that didn't work, he had a hundred per cent success with "And the worst part about it was" ......dramatic pause, "She was carrying my baby!"

Perhaps fortunately, the lads missed the arrival of

the American Airlines flight from Boston. Consolation was sought in the nearest bar which was in the International Hotel. There was still plenty of time to get to Limerick and collect Mareid. Inside the nearly empty bar, who did they meet but Rochie who they often drank with. He was overseeing a painting crew responsible for redecorating much of the hotel. Not wanting to be rude, Rochie accepted the offer of a pint and joined the lads for a chat about Munster rugby. Several pints later, again not wanting to be rude, Rochie invited his painting crew to join them.

Rochie was a wonderful story teller and immediately had them all in stitches. Sadly, the merriment was interrupted when a furious manager from the painting company marched in and interrupted Rochie just as he was reaching the punch line of his story. He was less than enthused by an annoyed Rochie's telling him to wait until he finished. The crew begrudgingly returned to their painting while Murphy and Tommy admiringly observed their artistry.

Attention then turned to a small group of middle aged Americans who had dropped in to sample the local brew and meet 'real' Irish people. Murphy instinctively knew he was moving close to the invisible line that would result in him waking up next day somewhere and not having a clue how he'd gotten there. Despite that and fleeting images of the lovely Mareid, he continued drinking.

For some unfathomable reason, their new Irish American friends delighted in Tommy's horrendous rendition of Galway Bay and insisted on another song from the bard. The Fields of Athenry had them weeping as they thought of their forefathers being forced off the land and emigrating to America to escape enforced poverty and famine. Not wanting to burst their bubble, Murphy settled back to enjoy the spectacle of Tuneless Tommy regaling his enraptured audience. Tommy was decent on the tin whistle but ridiculous when singing. Matters were not helped by

Rochie and the painting crew roaring encouragement. "Fair play to you boy! Go on Tommy raise the roof!"

A tall surly manager in his formal suit charged into the bar insisting all the unseemly noise be immediately stopped. Murphy heartily agreed with him. He was getting a headache from the brutal assaults Tommy had made on delightful Irish airs. Rarely the center of attention, Tommy took exception to this interruption to his riveting show. Having palled around with Tommy for some time and knowing of his capacity to clear a dance hall in minutes when he wanted to, Murphy felt concern for the annoyed manager.

"I'll sing a couple more then we'll be off," Tommy reasonably offered.

"No, you vil stop now." The manager didn't quite give a Nazi salute but vigorously punched his fist on the palm of his hand for emphasis.

Murphy wondered where the nearest hospital was. Tommy surprised him by smiling, "Come on Murph. Let's go outside. They've lovely fish there." Clueless to the fish reference, an intrigued Murphy and the Boston delegation followed Tommy outside.

A pond lay surrounded by plants and full with a wide assortment of exotic fish Murphy didn't recognize. Tommy, resplendent in his five hundred punt suit, laughed hysterically. He clumsily dived into the pond, immediately dislodging a confused carp. Murphy impulsively followed. The two of them laughed their arses off at the silliness of it all. Their American friends were delighted and couldn't wait to get home to Boston and tell of their time with the wild Irish back in the old country.

The Pied Piper crawled out of the pond, took out his tin whistle, and played a tune while Murphy and the Americans followed in a disorderly line. Dripping all over the expensive carpet, with the occasional fish falling from him, Tommy triumphantly led his devotees back into the bar, a grin as wide as the Shannon River imprinted on his face. "Ten pints and ten Hennessy please."

"Sorry, Tommy. The boss told me not to serve you now or ever."

Murphy silently groaned. In a heartbeat, this could get ugly.

A cherubic Tommy understood the bartender's position and, much to the delight of Rochie, his crew, and the enthralled Americans, Tommy began to pour the pints.

Murphy didn't know how it started, but suddenly the German and a rough looking group of lads appeared shouting evacuation instructions. Two of them were unceremoniously dropped by five foot three inches Tommy. The Irish American alliance was not found wanting. No one was going to mess with their friend Tommy! The invaders were quickly repelled. Tommy then got keys from the bar and locked the entrance so he would suffer no further interruption while consolidating Irish American relationships.

Murphy knew the police would soon arrive and suggested a prompt departure would be wise. "We'll have one for the road in Durty Nelly's," he suggested as enticement.

After impassioned requests to visit them in America, offers of accommodation, jobs, even daughters to marry, addresses and phone numbers were hastily exchanged on bar napkins. Then the lads, moments before the Gardai began banging on the bar door urged on by the frantic German, departed from a side exit and made their way back to Limerick. But first, a quick stop at Dirty Nelly's!

That was all Murphy remembered. He never collected Mareid or went to the school party. Instead, he awoke somewhere unfamiliar in the middle of the night while puking his guts out. Two days later, after searching all over Limerick, he finally discovered his car parked outside a pub near the Treaty Stone.

Chapter Sixteen

CHARITY FOR THE POOR

The clack of his leather shoes echoed as he walked across the sparkling marble floor then up the winding staircase. He was wearing a heavy leather overcoat. The matching gray woolen scarf covering his neck had been inadequate protection against the arctic winter winds that angrily howled outside. Despite being indoors, when blowing on his leather gloves, his breath formed an uneven cloud that drifted upwards. This would be his first meeting at the St. Vincent de Paul Society. He was feeling apprehensive because, at eighteen, he would be the youngest by far attending the meeting.

Cornelius Hannagan, family friend, prominent auctioneer, pillar of society, had recently approached Murphy at an Old Crescent rugger game and suggested he join the society. Since all his school friends had left Limerick and gone to college, Murphy had free time on his hands, so why not?

He heard voices and laughter from above, and sure enough, two floors later he entered a room big enough to seat fifty people. A mahogany table about twenty feet long and with eight matching chairs sat quietly waiting, and a pair of elegant chandeliers sprinkled light over the room and the three men warming themselves in front of a roaring coal fire. Red and gold reflected from their faces. Two were bent over laughing while vigorously rubbing their hands. Cornelius was there, as was Gerry Ryan and Louis McCarthy. Each of them had attended Crescent Jesuit so were welcomed members of the Old Crescent rugby club. Only boys who had attended Crescent Jesuit School were allowed membership. It helped keep out the riff raff.

Cornelius waved enthusiastically to him. "Ah, there he is, the lad himself. Welcome Brother Murphy, welcome!" His bushy eyebrows jumped up and down in delight and his eyes twinkled without blinking while his face opened wide with a smile that would melt winter away. His shiny head carried the unmarked face of a young man, even though he was fifty if he was a day, but that was where his fountain of youth ended. An explosion of chins wandered in quivering, uncontrolled motion all over his neck, and urgently strained for release behind the starched white shirt and blue striped Old Crescent club tie his mother had pressed for him earlier in the day. His breasts and tummies stuck way out making Murphy think of an over-inflated balloon that at any moment might float up to the ceiling. His hands were big, yet soft and puffy, and he continuously wrung them as he talked. He was unmarried, would remain unmarried, and lived with his adoring mother who could never be accused of underfeeding her man child.

He strolled across the room with hands outstretched, and put a pudgy arm around Murphy's shoulder, squeezing it tightly, before bringing him over to the warmth of the fire and introducing him to the other Brothers. "You know Brother Gerry and Brother Louis, don't you?"

Murphy nodded and smiled. Gerry Ryan's family, one of the wealthiest in town, had owned the local flour mills forever. It was well known that, even though Gerry occasionally dropped into the mill and had some fancy managerial title, he didn't work there. His passion lay in racehorses. He owned several thoroughbreds and raced them throughout the country. In fact, a horse of his had won at Cheltenham a few years back at twenty to one odds. He'd tipped off some school friends who then hired a plane to go over to England where they all made a killing. A permanent smile was etched on Gerry's unlined face. He possessed a quizzical look which seemed to always be wondering where he might find the next chance for fun.

Brother Louis offered a startling contrast. He was a chartered accountant who constantly fidgeted and rarely smiled. He moved away from the fire and Murphy briefly wondered if he was disturbed about the scandalous waste of coal. Or perhaps he was concerned that any sign of comfort might be interpreted by God as a sign he was having far too much fun on earth. Such frivolity would surely go on the debit side of the ledger against him when his book of life was eventually audited.

"You're no stranger to us, Brother Murphy," said Gerry with a smile that rivaled the Auctioneer's. "That was a great game you had in the semifinal of the Munster cup last year. Another five minutes and you'd have won."

Brother Louis, who stood stiff as a poker, barely nodded before lowering his wintry eyes. A suspicion of what might perhaps eventually become a tight smile almost forced itself onto his ridged face.

Another member bustled in, his energy overwhelming the room. "Evening Brothers!" boomed Tom Walsh, a leading barrister in the region. He was a former President of Rotary and had chosen Murphy's father as his vice president.

"Hello. How's your father and all the family?" In accordance with tradition, when growing up Murphy would never have dared call him by his first name, had always called him Mr. Walsh. He wondered what he was to address him by now. No need to respond since, without waiting for an answer, Mr. Walsh moved on. "Good. Good. Hello, Brothers. All right. Let's call the meeting to order." He charged over to the table, while the others dutifully followed.

"Before we start, Mr. President, I'd like to introduce a new member," announced a proud Cornelius.

"Think we all already know Murphy," responded Mr. Walsh gruffly.

Undeterred, Brother Cornelius beamed and continued, "Oh, indeed, Brother President, shur his family is well known and respected in the town and Murphy finished at the Crescent a few months ago. Now he's working at the Royal Insurance Group where our Brother George O'Connor is his manager. I was delighted to persuade Murphy to join us in our good works." He put his arm around Murphy and squeezed harder than earlier.

"You're more than welcome, Brother. Since this is your first meeting we'll team you up with a senior Brother to visit the poor."

Proprietary Cornelius adopted a nurturing paternal tone. "I brought him into the Society, Brother President, so I'll take care of him tonight, if that's all right with you." Everybody except Mr. Walsh beamed as they observed their nervous new brother.

"In the name of the Father, the Son, and the Holy Ghost," began the President with head bowed. The other Brothers closed their eyes, clasped their hands, and solemnly bowed their heads. Murphy reluctantly followed their example. Unless he escaped from Ireland, he was condemned to forever be in rooms where people blindly prayed. He'd given up that nonsense two years before, concluding that, although a brilliant business model, organized religion was a form of carefully orchestrated, mental insanity. The unquestioned, devotion to the God of his middle school years had died, making him nauseated whenever organized religion was mentioned. Looking up he found Brother Cornelius's eyes coldly fixed on him.

Finally, the praying was done, and the meeting continued with the secretary reading minutes from the previous week's meeting in a laborious, monotonous tone. "Five of the Brothers attended the meeting of November

13th. Present were Brothers Ryan, Duffy, Murphy, MacNeice, and Wallace. Brothers Gaynor and Lyons sent their apologies. Brother Duffy was in favor of giving a coal voucher to the O'Neill family in St. Mary's parish. They have eight children and another due any day. Any comments about that, Brothers?" The secretary looked up briefly from behind thick glasses that balanced precariously near the end of his very long nose, which housed a mighty pimple ripe for the plucking.

"Well," puffed Brother Cornelius, "The father is supposedly in England looking for work, but we can't be sure about that. Mrs. Reilly from two doors down tells us that he's not in England at all, and he always drinks his dole money before poor Mrs. O'Neill can get her hands on it. Apart from all that, whenever we visit the house and O'Neill is there, his attitude is most disrespectful to the Brothers. It's not just to me, I've checked with other Brothers, and they confirm what I'm saying. God knows we don't expect any gratitude for doing our corporal works of mercy, but at the same time we shouldn't have to tolerate obnoxious behavior from those we're volunteering to help. Two of the O'Neill children died in the past year. God knows, the poor creatures are much better off in heaven." He raised his eyes to the ceiling before deciding. "It's a sad and deserving case. So, despite, or because of, the father, I'm recommending a coal voucher, and vouchers for two pairs of children's shoes."

Other Brothers nodded agreement. Murphy wondered about the objectivity of decisions made to determine who would get the food, clothing, and coal. The secretary continued. "Brother Ryan recommended a food voucher to the value of five pounds and a pair of shoes for one of the Murphy children at 12 Prospect Road. Brother Regan recommends "no" to a request for clothes vouchers for the Driscoll family at 124 Clifford Road, Jamesboro. One of the neighbors tells us that Tommy Driscoll is working under the table and gets up to ten pounds a week from whatever work he is doing on the side. On top of that, he gets his dole money. We have several other more deserving cases."

Murmurs of agreement passed from the other Brother's mouths. Mrs. Driscoll's request for children's clothing was denied.

"And finally," concluded the secretary licking his dry lips, "our collection last week yielded five pounds fifty pence."

"Now if there is no objection I move to have the minutes approved," said the Barrister anxious to get to his next meeting.

Brother MacNeice raised his hand. "Proposed by Brother MacNeice."

"Mr. President, why don't we have our newest member second the motion," suggested the auctioneer.

"Splendid idea, Brother."

Murphy felt himself blushing while responding in a subdued manner. "I second the motion."

The Brothers nodded approval.

"Motion seconded by Brother Murphy. The minutes are approved."

"Finally, some general notes," continued the President. "The Society's national convention will be held in Galway next year. In March, I believe. We'll want a few members to travel so please think it over and talk with me during the next few weeks if anybody is interested in going as a delegate. The Peter's Pence collection will be held next Sunday week after the ten and twelve o'clock masses. We'll need to have two of our members at the collection boxes for each mass. Any volunteers?"

Brothers Louis and Cornelius predictably raised their hands. Murphy had a rugby match with Old Crescent, and Brother Ryan would be away at the Listowel races.

"Well if there's no other business," Mr. President

paused, "No? I want to welcome Brother Murphy into our little group. I expect to see him playing as out-half for Old Crescent this season and winning the Munster Senior cup for us." Murphy's new band of Brothers cheered and yelped like overgrown schoolboys at a wild party.

"Now we'll have the collection before I declare this meeting adjourned."

A leather bag was passed around into which private contributions were placed. Apart from the clinking of Murphy's few bob, the other contributions were silent.

The President rushed off to attend his next meeting at the Limerick Golf club. Brothers' Russell and MacNeice headed off together while Murphy accompanied Brother Cornelius. As they walked to his car, he contentedly hummed a Gilbert and Sullivan tune while Murphy followed closely in his wake.

It was a ten-minute drive over to Jamesboro, one of the places in Limerick where poor people lived. Murphy was about to be exposed to the dark underbelly of the class structure. Many of the workers from his father's factory lived in Jamesboro. Brother Cornelius turned right by the railway station and continued just up the hill from Carey's bar to where the corporation houses began. The houses were lined uncomfortably against each other in tightly packed rows, one pushing up against the next, small, and fragile with an ugly sense of desperation cloaking all of them.

Then Brother Cornelius began to pontificate with great seriousness, "You're going to see some things that will shock you. So, for tonight, simply watch me and see how it's done. Fair enough?" He reassuringly patted Murphy's knee when parking his car.

It was colder than usual that night with a bitter, glistening frost on the road. Despite being careful, they kept slipping and sliding on the broken footpath. They pulled the collars of their overcoats up over freezing necks. Their breath became fog rising over them as they walked toward the first poor house. Looking around, Murphy noticed there was no smoke coming from any chimney. "They must be freezing in those houses with no heat."

"Oh, it's terrible, awful," shook Cornelius's clearly distressed patrician head. "And, you know Murphy, we do what we can to help, but we can only do so much with our limited resources. But it's not all gloom and doom for them. Although they endure hardships, these people get their houses rent free. They also get free milk, dole money and whatever the other agencies, and we, can help with. And many of them work when there's jobs to be had. In some ways, they have advantages we can never hope to enjoy. They don't have to stay awake all night worrying about the economy, paying mortgages, running a business, taxes, and so much more. I'm not saying I'd prefer their lifestyle, God knows, it's not easy, but all I'm saying is, that in some ways, it's not as bad as it appears and could always be worse. So much of life is a series of tradeoffs. You'll find that as time goes by." He said it in a way that seemed somewhat melancholy, but finding humor somewhere, he laughed again, "Ah sure, it's good for the soul!"

Murphy had no idea what the Brother was talking about. It was hard to visualize any benefit to being poor, especially trying to stay alive on miserably cold winter nights such as that one. He recalled his mother and he, on many an occasion, huddled round the blazing fire at home, hands outstretched trying to trap its warmth, and this mother saying, "God help those unfortunate poor people in Limerick tonight who have no fire or heat." Pointless sharing his thoughts since Cornelius seemed to find poverty to have appealing, almost virtuous qualities.

"We begin here with the Jackson family and have two other families to visit who are requesting our assistance," smiled the Brother as they approached the door of 181

Victoria Terrace, Jamesboro. "This case, the Jackson family, is especially sad. A social worker, who's also one of our members, told me that one of the young girls who recently had a baby admitted that her father is the baby's father. Mrs. Jackson refuses to turn him in, and the local parish priest understandably won't do anything to break up the marriage. "

It took Murphy's innocent mind a few seconds to grasp what had been said, and by then he was knocking on the Jackson's door that was broken and didn't close properly. It was held in place by a mangy piece of brown twine that failed to adequately block out most of the wind that demanded entry. Two missing panes of glass had been replaced by cardboard portraying faded pictures of happy children playing in summer fields. Another pane was splintered; but one remained in good condition. Inside, a man and woman cursed each other, while children cried and screamed. Cornelius threw his eyes up to heaven before knocking louder.

By now they'd been heard, and everybody, except a baby, immediately shut up. Murphy imagined the sign language and shushing going on behind the door. A moment later a hand came out and undid the string.

"Ah sure hello, Mr. Hannagan, an anoder gintleman," welcomed a scrawny woman with a wrinkled, beaten up face. Around her body was a black shawl that failed to cover a belly full with child.

"Hello there, Bridie," beamed the Auctioneer. "Hello, Paddy," to a man sitting with a fiddle under his arm.

Murphy recognized him. It was Jackson. He used work in the packing department at his father's factory but had an accident one day when a pallet, laden down with nails and screws, fell and smashed his leg. It never healed properly, so he couldn't work anymore, either at the factory or anywhere else. Nowadays he still walked with a heavy limp. But he was great at playing the fiddle and, apart from the dole, that was how he earned extra money. On many a day, he'd be found outside Woolworth's in O'Connell Street playing a lively tune while a tinker friend of his, with a black patch over one eye, strummed the banjo in accompaniment in between asking for donations.

"This is Mr. Murphy, one of the Society's new members. New young blood, Mrs. Jackson, that's what the Society needs, right?" And he slapped Murphy yet again hard across his shoulder. But Murphy's attention was elsewhere. He couldn't take his eyes off a young girl, thirteen, maybe fourteen at most, lying in the corner, trying to feed her father's retarded, bastard child who was drooling a heavy mixture of snot and hungry tears.

"Hellow, Mr. Murphy." Jackson looked sheepishly up, smiling with crocked face in belated recognition.

A few two years previously, at the factory Christmas draw, Murphy's father had him drawing tickets out of a barrel, and he'd drawn one of Jackson's tickets, then presented him with a plump turkey. Murphy felt uncomfortable meeting him again under these circumstances. It made him realize that, but for the vagaries of fate, their places could have been reversed.

He counted at first six then seven other children in the room. Some lay on the floor in makeshift resting places that served as beds. Peeling blue wallpaper hung from one wall, while the remainder was painted chalky white. The fireplace was in darkness; long-dead ashes pushed to the side. A large wooden box had been converted into a table and three of the children were hunched over it as they finished eating Matterson's beans from a can while sharing a piece of cold, dry bread.

The wind from the front door blew winter inside but, despite the cold, the children didn't have many clothes on. They looked up at the warm way the brothers were dressed.

Murphy felt ashamed of his leather gloves and heavy overcoat with matching woolen scarf. One child stared past them with expressionless eyes. The others lay on the makeshift beds, motionless, like refugees in a war zone. Murphy wondered what it was like to live in that hellhole, day after day, with all the mental, physical, and social abuse constantly assaulting their senses. The children looked miserable, scared, and hungry. The room itself was reasonably clean. Cracked dishes and cups were washed and drying in the sink but there was still the unavoidable stench of neglect and poverty. Murphy realized these children were condemned to a life of hopelessness. He was reminded of the Irish famine paintings from the 1830's that showed women with arms outstretched, starving children clutching their tattered skirts, while their mothers begged for bread to feed them.

The way Cornelius talked down to these people disgusted Murphy. His patronizing tone was repulsive to Murphy. The woman wasn't much better, with all her fawning "Gintleman" bullshit. Irish people had been beaten down throughout history and had inherited the habit of cowering before their superiors. So, there was this broken woman, talking subserviently to Brother Cornelius, the overfed Lord of the m who would hopefully sprinkle a few crumbs into the mouths of the dispossessed.

"If ye could see to it, Sir, dat we git a food an coal voucher we'd be more dan grateful. Haven't had no vouchers for monts now, and wit a new baby about t'arrive any day, tanks be ta God, is dare any way de good Society and yourself could see to it for us ta get de vouchers, and de blessings of our Lady, de Virgin Mary, on boat of you fine gintlemen." She coquettishly smiled a lop-sided grin, displaying a practically toothless mouth with bleeding gums. Then, she lowered her gaze to below the Auctioneer's feet in an action of absolute servitude, and respectfully awaited his reaction.

Cornelius adopted a pensive air, opened his arms wide as if blessing an attentive congregation, then closed them again before winking over at Murphy. "I don't know, Mr. Murphy, what do you think? Sure, Jackson here probably earns more in a week than you and me would in a month, eh, Jackson?" and he roared laughing while gleefully clapping his hands together and rocking back and forth on the balls of his feet.

"Oh, I doubt dat very much now, Sir," responded Jackson playing the game well, sitting cross-legged on a box as he dug deep in his pocket for a nobber to smoke. He reeked of booze and fags while muttering something under his breath.

"And wouldn't we only be encouraging Jackson here to drink all his money as he usually does, eh, eh, Mr. Murphy?"

By now Mr. Jackson, Mrs. Jackson and most of the children were also laughing and everybody was having a grand old time.

Abruptly adopting a more serious tone, Brother Cornelius closed his eyes and raised his hand giving absolution like the priest he never would be. "I'll promise you nothing tonight, Mrs. Jackson. The matter must go before the entire committee and we can only do so much. But rest assured, and I'm sure I can speak here for Mr. Murphy, that we will recommend supporting you in these matters."

"Oh, tank you, Sir, an God bless youse boat. May all of yer sons be Bishops."

The good work completed, their leather gloves shook hands with the Jackson family and hastily left. The family all stood in the cold, smiling and waving goodbye as the Brothers disappeared into the drifting fog that swirled around the houses. Turning on the heater, Cornelius looked over and asked, "Well, what do you think?"

Perhaps wisely, Murphy didn't immediately respond.

His head was whirling with conflicting emotions. He'd seen more desperation and sadness in those few minutes, than he had in his entire life. "I think I'm not cut out for this. Never saw anything more depressing. And the young girl with the baby? And the mother with another baby on the way, Jesus Christ, it's horrendous." Despite the freezing night that it was, he opened the window and breathed in the cold air, trying as best he could to erase the smell of piss and misery that still clung to his clothes.

"I know, I know," Cornelius sighed as if the weight of the world rested heavily on his fragile shoulders. "It's always hard, especially when you first get exposed to their life, but it's important not to get emotionally involved. If you do that, you lose all sense of objectivity and that's no good to anyone now, is it?"

But Murphy found it impossible to dispel the images of those emaciated, doomed children. Their terrified faces kept floating before his eyes. They were subhuman species; living corpses, barely breathing, as they lay watching the Brothers. They had neither pride of ancestry nor hope of succession to anything other than the squalid room that imprisoned them.

The remaining two visits weren't as bad, but he was still shocked at the horrific living conditions, if they could correctly be called that, of all these families. When their good deeds had been completed the Brothers headed towards Murphy's home. He felt relief flooding through him the farther they drove from that part of town, past the railway station, then over by People's park, the Barrington Street side of which was graced with magnificent, red bricked Georgian houses where many doctors, barristers and dentists had their offices. Then down Summerville Avenue to his home. Cornelius parked further down the avenue where he had darkness and total privacy.

He put his hand on Murphy's knee then quickly

moved it upwards. A horrified Murphy pushed him away. He finally broke the awkward silence by asking "Will the committee approve the Jackson's application?"

"They would if we recommended it. That's why we have a great responsibility. We must be sure to give to the most deserving cases and watch that we're not fooled. No, I don't think we'll recommend the Jackson family. He can always make an extra few bob if they're really stuck by playing the fiddle outside Woolworth's, and then there's always his dole money if she gets any of it. We've got to be careful not to support their boozing. She drinks her fair share as well, you know, and is often seen with some of the children sitting down begging on O'Connell Street outside the Augustinians. She's very good at it I hear. God knows I'm no prude, and I like a good time as much as the next man, but he always reeks of porter every time I meet him. No, there are clearly more deserving cases, but sadly the Jackson's are beyond our help. Now the Hogans, the last family we visited, a really deserving case. Two of the children are making their First Holy Communion next week. They will need shoes for the ceremony, and some coal for the celebration in the house later. Are Old Crescent playing away this weekend?"

While laying in bed that night, Murphy decided to resign from the Society. Next day he posted a letter to the President. Two days later, Brother Cornelius repeatedly called him, both at work and at home, demanding an explanation for Murphy's sudden resignation. "Sorry. I'm uncomfortable doing this type of volunteer work. It's different to what I'd anticipated."

His parents were disappointed he was no longer involved with the Society. They believed it was a worthy cause, and would be beneficial for business connections. Murphy listened on an extension phone while Cornelius consoled them, explaining that, "Just as not everyone is called by God to the priesthood, not everyone is cut out to do the Society's challenging work."

Chapter Seventeen

STREAKING

"Caff, this is your last chance to do a runner," Murphy explained to his friend who was about to willingly enter the counter intuitive institution of marriage. There were four of the lads having a drink in Dirty Nellies. Caff, Murphy, Edi, and Rashers, all resplendent in tuxedos and corresponding attitudes.

"Fuck off, Murph." Caff laughed, his love-struck face lost to any form of reasoned logic that might save him. Time had run out for him. He bought another round while smiling happily at the thought of finally bedding Mary Ryan whom he'd hotly pursued for the prior three years. The lads rarely discussed sex, especially where girlfriends were concerned, but Murphy doubted if Caff had got very far with his bride-to-be. He'd bet a pound to a penny she was still a virgin. Ironically, Caff was a wonder with women. They went mad for his good looks and genuinely happy disposition. He'd always had any woman he fancied; now he was marrying the virgin Mary. Had he known the future he could have turned his back and avoided the tragedy.

"Slainte"

"Slainte maith." Brandies swirled in the glasses. Sniffing the aroma, the lads knocked them back.

They'd known each other all their lives, had spent years in small classrooms at the Crescent. Murphy had known Annie since she was a baby. But now Caff was getting married to her. He was the first of the lads to go. The inevitable domino effect was not lost on Murphy. The lads were breaking up. Within the next few hours, Caff would be gone from them. "Drink." Murphy frantically urged, "For tomorrow we die!"

Despite more wasted entreaties, the wedding happened; lashings of good liquor and excellent food were downed with wines that tasted lovely, all of them. After Caff and his bride had left and the wedding party quieted down, the rest of the lads headed off to county Clare for some traditional Irish music. Among others, the great fiddle player, Packi Russell, was playing in Doolin; so, the craic went on well into the night and until light slowly rose up from the Atlantic.

They moved on to Kilkee, still dressed in what was left of their tuxedos. Two days later they headed back to Limerick and their local pub, the "Gates of Hell." It was called that because it was down an alleyway behind the Augustinian church.

By then they were knackered; an exhausted mess of depraved youth. But some pretty girls in the bar provided temporary fuel, so when a conversation turned to the latest craze called streaking, and a fifty-pound wager was placed, Murphy jumped at the challenge. The rules were that he was to strip naked in the bar, run up the alleyway, down by Thomas Street and round by Catherine Street where the taxi ranks were, then up O'Connell and around by the alleyway back into the pub. Tom Hickey was to run with him to make sure that he had covered the agreed territory.

Accompanied by catcalls, whistling, and banging of pint glasses on tables, he stripped naked and did a Charles Atlas impression before being pushed out into the street. Murphy could see the police barracks outside the Gates of Hell and noticed one of the Garda Shiocana had unfortunately spotted him, so off he charged with Tommy Hickey in quick pursuit and the Garda following behind. He was a beefy lad and Murphy figured he wouldn't last long. Sure enough, after covering an enthusiastic half mile the Garda pulled up. Murphy looked back, and saw him clutching his belly as he leaned his arm against a Volkswagen that had two dignified old ladies sitting in it. Murphy almost collapsed from laughing when he saw the horrified expressions on their faces as the policeman puked all over their windshield.

He turned down Thomas Street where all the taxi drivers started honking their horns and cheering wildly, delighted with the craic. By then the Gardai from the William Street Station were on full alert to the disgraceful conduct of civil disorder and a squad of them rushed out of the barracks hoping to end Murphy's disgraceful behavior.

He was half way down O'Connell when he was horrified to see his mother who was coming closer with every millisecond. Then she was standing less than fifty yards away, talking to Monsignor Reilly, smiling up at him with broad smile, delighted that he was talking with her. Inexplicably, Murphy wondered if she was asking him about how long the soul stayed in the body after death. She'd been worried sick about it since their next-door neighbor had died one night a few months before from a heart attack and it had taken the priest two hours to arrive and give him the sacrament of the last rites.

Mother and the monsignor were distracted by the sounds of women screaming, men shouting, children cheering, and cars honking. They craned their necks to see what caused the commotion and then they saw Murphy, unshaven, hair flying, completely starkers, coming at breakneck speed towards them with his jewels flapping wildly and uncontrollably in every direction, and beefy Gardai with batons raised shouting like Keystone cops, charging to catch the disgusting, disturber of the peace. Murphy felt like someone about to witness a train wreck. There would be hell to pay for this. He heard the shouts of the police and then, before him, was his misfortunate mother, her arm resting on the Monsignor's, the other hand on her forehead as she observed the madman approaching her. She almost fainted when the recognition of her youngest child's face hit her brain. Her body slumped back against the Monsignor who was having his own problems as he hastily fondled his rosary beads and repeated, "Oh, sweet Jesus, Merciful hour, merciful hour." All Murphy could think of ridiculously saying as he sped by was, "Afternoon mother. Hello Monsignor."

His horrified mother lowered her head, her hands falling dejectedly to her sides. She looked distraught and humiliated. Tom Hickey followed closely. "Hello, Mrs. Murphy!" he shouted while Murphy's mother, with jaw around her ankles, watched several Gardaí charge past roaring for her naked son to stop and surrender. But by then, Murphy had gone around the corner with just one block to safety. He dashed down the alleyway to be met with great applause as he fell through the doors of the Gates of Hell.

Dressing himself as quickly as possible, completely knackered, he enthusiastically drowned a pint of Harp. His face was puffed and sweaty. Being on the piss for three days and nights had taken its toll. He took the fifty pounds, handed it to the barman to buy drinks for everyone until it was all gone.

He'd just begun another pint when the Gardaí Shiochana came charging in the door, three brave lads, all panting badly. They looked around the now silent bar with amused drinkers anticipating the outcome. Scanning the crowd, they pushed their way through before standing inches from Murphy's flushed and sweating face. "Ye were seen performin an illegal act in public, contrary of several statutes."

They were big lads, definitely from down the country, and not the sort of lads you'd want to give an excuse to use their batons. "Sorry, Officer, there must be some mistake.

I've been here at this bar for the past four hours and haven't moved except to go for the occasional piss."

"Ye were not, ya liar. I chased you all de way round."

"Officer, all you probably saw of the person you chased was his arse. Now, you're not going to ask me to take down my pants for a sort of arse line up, are you?"

"Smart little bollix aren't ye!" He made a lunge at Murphy who jumped out of his way as a Garda banged into the girlfriend of one of the local hard chaws who did not appreciate his girlfriend's head hopping off the wall. He head butted the Garda whose nose was heard to crack. Blood dribbled down his chin. A quiet girl who had said not a word all morning suddenly grabbed a bottle of whiskey and declared the battle cry, "Fuckin' Pigs," in either an American or Canadian accent. She threw the bottle at the other policemen who had by now been joined by even more of the lads from the nearby barracks. This was a small bar, usually seating thirty at most, but they were at least forty-five and everybody freaking out, the lads mostly plastered, the girls with hands pulling hair, screaming their heads off and, of course, loving all the drama. The Gardai were understandably furious. Batons began to fly, and had the pub had not been so crowded many more bones and teeth would have been broken. As it was, nothing should have happened. It wasn't necessary. Just a bit of innocent craic.

Murphy managed to scramble out a side door then away with Tom Hickey and him around the corner. They slowed down, then meandered up Thomas Street towards the railway station and into Patsy Naughton's for steak with lashings of spuds and unions. They cracked up telling Patsy what had happened and he loved it. He brought his wife out and insisted Murphy retell the story in every detail, then refused to take any money. "I'm getting the better of the deal," he said as more tears fell into the fryer cooking the chips.

Murphy finally struggled home, very quietly made it to his bedroom then crashed for a full rotation of the planet.

Next evening, he wanted to avoid his mother but unsuccessfully avoided dinner. The atmosphere was very strained. Nobody spoke a word. After eating, father and son went into the living room. Soon his mother handed over two steaming hot cups of Barry's tea as the men warmed themselves before the fire. His mother wordlessly went back to the kitchen. He could hear her cleaning up, and washing dishes. Eventually she returned with a fresh brew of tea. A bright red tea cozy covered the pot which she placed beside an assortment of Boland's biscuits. She left it untouched for a few minutes to draw properly, then carefully poured a strong cup for his father, then Murphy and finally herself.

The fire needed some life, so his father shoveled more fuel on it. The broken pieces of coal hissed like angry serpents as he carefully placed turf from the farm in Kildare on top. The unique flavor of turf cast its spell on them. His father proudly claimed, "It's the best fire smell you'll ever get. Turf from the bog of Allen."

As they silently sat listening to the radio while sipping tea, Murphy was about to burst with the tension of waiting for someone to speak about his streaking. Although it had seemed pure inspiration, the novelty had long worn off. Although his father rarely spoke of his upbringing, Murphy knew it had been tough with zero time for frivolity. Being the eldest child of eleven from a working-class Dublin family, he had been like a second father helping his mother raise all those children. There was no time for him to have a fun youth. He had never known what it was like to be a youngster on the craic. Murphy suspected his father enjoyed the wild things he did, even if his son's behavior was reason for concern.

Still little was said as they sat around the fireplace. They sipped tea and laughed at the radio show called, "The

School Around the Corner." The room was now toasty from the glowing fire. Not much sound out on the avenue except the birds returning home to their trees for the night. Silence followed the end of the radio show as his father turned it off. Surely now his mother would bring the streaking out into the open. But that could be postponed if his father suggested they go to Fennessy's pub for a jar. Murphy could usually time his impending departure based on the way he moved his body. First his right foot would begin tapping, then he'd shift uneasily several times in his seat as if in great discomfort, look at his watch, tap it to make sure it was working, and say, "Good God, is that the time it is?" A shocked shake of the head was followed by, "Time to take the dog for a walk." The fact that we had no dog was immaterial. "So," his father looked over. "Do you want to go for a quick pint?"

Good man yourself! "I don't mind," Murphy tried to sound almost reluctant. If he could get out the door without his mother spilling the beans, he would be safe until tomorrow.

"Is there anything you want to say to your father?" she asked waving away the clouds of smoke to eyeball her disgraceful son.

"What's this about?" His father asked, his interest apparently piqued.

"No, nothing that won't hold 'till later. We won't be long." Murphy moved like a hare for the door as his father followed behind. His mother puffed away. They left the room with her sitting alone looking into the fire as the warmth in it began to die under her withering glare.

It was slippery going up the Avenue. They were mountain climbers clinging to the walls along the side to keep balance. It was better at the top where they turned right and the shadow of the Nun's Training College towered over them. Here trees standing forty feet tall protected the paths from any frost or ice and it was the same most of the way to Fennessy's public house. Murphy hadn't gone there for a while after a previous embarrassing situation unfolded involving a married woman, but habit is strong and this was their local pub his family had been going to since he was a baby.

When Murphy was seven his father had discretely pointed out a man sitting in a corner of the pub by himself. "He's a dentist and he's actually DIVORCED," his father had said, his tone rich in meaning. Murphy was shocked, didn't know that was possible in Ireland. He carefully sneaked a long look at the divorced man, since he'd never heard of, let alone seen, anybody who was divorced. "He doesn't do much business." His father added, with a slow, knowing nod of his head.

Now the sounds of friends greeted them. "Night, Michael, hardy old night." "'Tis indeed, but nothing a hot toddy can't take care of." "True for you." They went into the snug area. His father, as usual, insisted on buying the drinks. He'd never once allowed his brother or Murphy to buy a round. "So how was Caff's wedding? You were gone a few days. Must have been a long ceremony. Didn't realize you were so religious," he said in a deadpan, serious voice.

Ignoring the barb, Murphy instead told him vague details. He wondered should he tell him about the streak, but funked it since they'd moved on to having a grand ole chat about sports and plays he had been in with the College Players, and all the craic they'd had. He was about to tell another story, when in came members of Old Crescent rugby club. They spent the next two hours hotly debating the standard of local, provincial, and international rugby teams. There is no person in the rugby world as knowledgeable or passionate as a Limerick rugby man.

"Time, gentlemen, please, last call, last call please," Michael Fennesey called to his patrons.

"Get me a half one, will you. And whatever the lads

are having."

Murphy got up to get the drinks, was walking away from the table when his father shouted to his departing back, "I'd have given a small fortune to see your mother's, and especially the Monsignor's, faces when they realized it was you."

Laughter and guffaws loudly followed his father's declaration. Murphy looked back to see his father taking a bunch of Limerick Leader front pages from out of his coat and handing them to the lads. The headline read, "LIMERICK'S FIRST STREAKER! SON OF PROMINENT LIMERICK BUSINESSMAN STRIPS, STREAKS, THEN CAUSES RIOT IN BAR."

The rest of the group were shaking in convulsive laughter as they read the article. His father's laughing blue eyes sparkled fondly at Murphy and he raised his glass with indulgent salutation.

Chapter Eighteen

AFTERMATH

It was past midday before he finally crawled out of bed and reluctantly made his way downstairs. His mother was about to serve lunch. Her lips were sewn together so her mouth had disappeared. She sat rigidly upright at the silent lunch table as though bolted to the chair. The only sound was their cutting through the food and the chewing, followed by milk being gulped as it made its way down their throats.

Grim, with a furious scowl chiseled into her crumbling face, his mother resembled an unkempt, historical monument, once magnificent but now, beaten down by life and neglect, reduced to a cruel imitation of her former glory. She spent much of each day locked in her bedroom surrounded by pills and Gilbey's Gin she kept poorly hidden in her closet. Murphy was certain, as she stole him a furtive glance, that he could hear her heart pounding at an alarming rate, her blood, like a river about to break the levee, racing madly throughout her body ready to explode.

He sometimes wondered why his parents had married. His father always swore he thought, on his way to the church, it was his younger brother John who was marrying her. He claimed the outcome came as a complete shock to him. There he was, standing at the altar, quietly minding his own business, intending no harm to anybody, when he put out his hand to congratulate his brother, but suddenly it was he, and not his brother, who was wearing the wedding ring.

Murphy looked past his mother and observed his

father quietly working in the garden, doubtless imagining his land was a rural hideaway. As he toiled he surely dreamed about Kildare and life on the farm. He dug strongly, looking fit and trim, standing at over six foot one. His other son Liam, was over six-foot, and his daughter Grainne was also tall for a girl. Murphy had once heard it said that the best part of him must have run down his father's legs.

The farmer paused, rested his weight on his shovel, and glared up at the cold sun that hid behind thick banks of fat, motionless clouds. Taking off his cap and using his elbow to wipe away the sweat on his brow, he made this simple act seem an heroic gesture, man and Nature at peace with each other, nurturing the soil. He delighted in the healthy fresh vegetables, tomatoes, lettuce, rhubarb, and even giant green melons he produced in his city land. He was a laborer in the field, who had to be back wearing a suit at the office within the next half-hour. He waved to Murphy. They smiled at each other. He took a quick look at his watch then, moving with a greater sense of urgency, turned his attention back to the land.

Murphy wondered was his father realistic enough to enjoy the dream of being away from the factory and toiling in the fields from dawn to dusk, while remaining aware that he would go insane if stuck permanently on the remote farm with its hardships. He would also have to deal with his unhappy wife sitting shaking her head, looking forlornly out the window into the dreary mist and miserable Arctic weather.

Father's frequent but brief visits there were always enough to have him driving away feeling nostalgic, yet delighting in the knowledge that by nightfall he would end up at his comfortable urban home. He would arrive into Fennessy's pub in time for a few jars and dreamily regale his audience with stories about the joys of farming. "You know Lads, there's some unique quality about the land. We're just

passing through, but it'll be there long after we're all gone."
He'd sigh as the golden whiskey met his lips. By then he
usually had a decent share of drink on board, not to mention
what his sister Pearl would have poured into him before he'd
left Kildare. After the pub closed, he'd head home to Sutton.
There, he'd tumble into bed to enjoy, from the safety of his
centrally heated, lawn manicured, well-ordained habitat,
vivid dreams depicting his demanding, yet fulfilling life of
retirement on the farm.

It was when he returned from these trips that he
began to pull his wife's leg. They'd be sitting down for
dinner next day, and he'd start off, "Frank was showing me
a few acres going at the right price beside their place. What
do you think?" He'd have a deadly serious face on him while
simultaneously kicking Murphy under the table.

His wife would look at him as if he'd lost his marbles.
Very slowly and deliberately she'd say, "What-do-you-mean,
what-do-I-think?"

Murphy's father would then happily egg her on. "Ah,
I'm sick of the rat race. I expect we could settle everything
within the month, six weeks at most. Of course, it'd take at
least a year or two to build the house, so we'd have to live
with Pearl and Frank for most, if not all, of that time. And
sure," here he usually paused for effect, carefully cutting
his meat, covering it with spuds, butter, and rich gravy
before concluding, "The Ma is less than thirty miles away
in Dublin." Then he'd adopt a look of cherubic, childlike
innocence while looking out the window, oblivious to
everybody's presence, having wandered off into a dreamlike
state while still throwing the occasional kick at Murphy
who'd watch his mother and almost crack up from trying not
to laugh as her face turned several colors. She could handle
most things, including Pearl, if necessary, but to have her
husband's mother, the perfect woman, as she was adoringly
called by her nine sons, to have the Ma living so close and

always available for drop in! Well, that would be intolerable. She'd hold back for as long as she could, which wasn't very long, then she'd be lighting cigarette after cigarette before quickly disappearing under the usual cloud of smoke. "If you think," fire and spittle shooting from her mouth, "If you think I'm going to live in some remote bog where the nearest toilet is somewhere in the next county, you can forget it. I'm staying here." Then she adopted an incredulous posture, pulled her sweater tightly closed, and tugged the belt tighter. "Live with Pearl indeed!" Then, ignoring her husband, and talking directly to Murphy, "I'm very fond of Pearl, you know I am," she'd claim this, dripping sincerity, "but she's up at the crack of dawn every day, and I like to lie in a bit." She had absolutely no intention whatsoever in swapping her creature comforts to spend her remaining years traipsing around the bog of Allen in Wellington boots before dawn, with Aunt Pearl and herself up to their necks in cow muck.

At this statement his father's thick eyebrows quickly stood to attention before lowering to rest over his eyes. Then more cigarettes were lit and his wife continued to vigorously puff, horrified by this ghastly proposition she had already heard many times before. This scene, or variations on it, seemed to be a mad ritualistic dance around their emotions. The baiting and subsequent response happened enough to make Murphy wonder if, in some perverse way, this was simply a neurotic method for them to communicate on some level.

And his father did seem to care for her, showed it in small ways. Murphy wondered if his mother ever noticed. Along with most of Ireland, she always listened to the morning Gay Byrne radio show. His parents hadn't slept together since he was young and yet, despite that, his father came into her bedroom every morning, come hell or high water, with the Irish Times, a fresh cup of Barry's tea, with a little milk and one sugar, and well done crispy toast with a suggestion of orange marmalade sitting politely on melted butter. Gay Byrne didn't end until ten o'clock. Apart from some relatively minor energy used to sip her tea, and nibble on the toast, his mother never stirred until Gay said goodbye to her. That had been her morning routine for many years but, such was her bitterness, he'd never once heard her say thanks.

Murphy's daydreaming provided a brief respite from the inevitable. He was still in the dining room where his mother sat fuming and loudly silent. Beads of perspiration had formed on her forehead even though the room was cold. He watched as one drop jumped over her eyebrow then meandered down the side of her left cheek mixing with her make-up. She swiped impatiently at it. She knew damned well he was looking at her, but wouldn't respond.

Unable to handle the tension he decided to bring matters to a head. "We need to talk, there's no point in us sitting here like a pair of idiots ignoring each other."

She looked over, then away again, and mumbled, "I daren't think what your father will say when he hears about your most recent disgraceful performance." She glared briefly before looking away.

Murphy laughed it off. "For heaven's sake Mum, he knows. And it was only a bit of craic."

"That's certainly not what Monsignor O'Donnell thought!" Her face contorted into what seemed to be a smile before she collapsed into sobs while repeatedly shaking her head mortified at her disgrace.

Murphy felt bad for her but was clueless about what to do. "Look, I'm sorry I embarrassed you. As you know, we gave Caff a good send off. He was the first to go."

"You make it sound as if he's been executed," she shot back around the handkerchief she now wept into.

He wisely decided not to respond to that trapdoor. "Then we went on to County Clare to listen to Irish music for a few days. Yes, I admit things did get a bit out of hand," he laughed cheerfully, but his mother's face had turned from dark red to white as if all the blood had suddenly been drained from her body. Her usual ladylike demeanor disappeared as her fist banged on the table making her plate and silverware jump up in shock. "Did you say, a little out of hand? Do you consider disgracing your family, running like a madman, NAKED through the streets of Limerick for all the world to laugh at.....you consider that of no consequence?"

Murphy was at a loss how to respond. Then he made things worse. "It was only done for a bet. And I suppose I was a little bit drunk." They both knew that the "little" reference was a crock. By now, Murphy was feeling defensive and wanted one of them, preferably him, to get the hell out of the room.

"I'd suggest that you claiming to be "a little drunk" is like saying the Titanic took on a bit of water. God knows," she sighed dramatically, "I thought it was bad when you crashed into that Volkswagen last August. If we didn't have good connections, you'd have been sent to jail. And how you've kept your job I don't know. And then you brought that misfortunate girl Eileen home last month; taking advantage of her drunken state. But this most recent escapade of yours really takes the biscuit. It's like you've gone mad! I don't understand what's happened to you. God alone knows where you'll end up."

He was thrown off track by her bringing up the subject of the car crash, Eileen, his approaching madness, and her prophesy of his impending doom. He also lost his train of thought reconciling the idea of his taking advantage of "poor Eileen," but knew it was better to remain silent. Looking out the window he noticed his father had gone.

Silence at the table brought him back. "Would you like me to talk with the Monsignor?" he asked in a conciliatory tone.

"You'd be well advised to stay well away from the Monsignor. You almost gave the poor man a stroke, and with him barely a year away from retirement. Shame on you!" His mother stood up, and prepared to make her exit, glistening eyes still boring into her despicable son. She wondered who the stranger at her table was. Then the venom. "You're nothing but a continual source of embarrassment to the family."

"Well, you wouldn't allow me to emigrate to Australia last year even after you knew I was mad keen to leave Ireland, and had all the required papers. You didn't want to me leave this precious nest you've built. So, don't give me a hard time now. If you hadn't interfered, I could just as easily have been streaking in Sydney."

His mother froze momentarily, an animal caught in the headlights, then quickly summoned what little dignity remained. Still glaring daggers at her disgusting failure, she rose wearily, dragged her wounded spirit across the floor, and removed herself from her son's unworthy presence.

Chapter Nineteen

LEAVING HOME

Her head was about to explode into a thousand pieces. He stepped back to avoid the fallout. "How DARE you submit your resignation letter without first discussing it with your father and me!"

It was a warm September evening as he nervously delivered the news. What he didn't dare tell her was he'd left the company two weeks before. Hiding that reality, each morning he'd get up as usual, eat the breakfast she'd prepared for him, put on his suit, take his brief case and black umbrella, then leave. He'd wave goodbye as she carefully watched his departure while offering a regal wave of her own from behind the usual cloud of cigarette smoke.

The pubs wouldn't be open until ten so he'd sit at the Galleon restaurant in O'Connell Street patiently drinking tea. His regular order of Barry's tea, toast and marmalade was always brought to him within minutes of his arrival. Then he'd spend the day going into several pubs as he didn't want anyone to think he was drinking too much. Sitting alone in the Lyric or Savoy film theaters and visits to the bookies filled the rest of his time. He felt relieved at no longer having to get up with a hangover and face another meaningless work day with the insurance company.

But now his mother glared with disgust at her disappointment of a son before pointedly dismissing him with an ominous, "Wait till your father hears about this."

He'd been working for a year as an insurance clerk with the Royal Insurance Group in Mallow Street. No one had any doubt he was fun but also incredibly incompetent, a day dreamer who would never have held down the job were it not for the value of his father's account to the insurance company.

He didn't endear himself to the company hierarchy when one of them, Gordon Rycroft, was visiting the colony. He asked Murphy's opinion about the company training program he'd attended in Hoylake, Cheshire. Murphy enthusiastically espoused his ideas on how to improve the sadly lacking course. While doing so he noticed his manager, Mr. George O'Connor, frantically waving his arms behind the home office gentleman. An uncomfortable silence followed before a clearly aggrieved Gordon Rycroft was hastily led away for an early, liquid lunch. The training restructuring had been his brain child. Murphy had attended the first class.

Part of his job was to take orders over the phone, mainly from farmers in the west of Ireland who needed coverage for their machinery and cars. He was supposed to quote, arrange payment, and then send them a temporary notice of coverage. Unfortunately, he easily became distracted and forgot to fill the orders. His solution was to dump many incomplete files into a box he kept hidden under his desk. He'd regularly receive frantic calls from anxious farmers demanding to know where their certificates of insurance were. Many would have been stopped by the police and were required to produce proof of coverage. When that happened he'd simply write up a certificate, back date the date of cover, then send it out to the much-relieved farmers.

His filing system worked successfully until he returned from a friend's wedding after being absent while on a tear for three days after the reception. Mr. George O'Connor called him into his office for an ominous chat.

"A good time at the wedding yes?"

"Ah, grand altogether Mr. O'Connor. Grand."

"Good. Well, that's good, isn't it?"

An uncomfortable silence followed while they looked blankly at each other. Murphy knew he was in trouble but had no idea specifically what it might be, and had no intention of making the imminent bollicking any easier for Mr. O'Connor.

Sighing heavily, he reached under his desk and produced Murphy's unique filing system. Murphy vaguely remembered shredding files prior to the wedding but couldn't remember to what extent. Mr. O'Conner pushed the box away, as if it was toxically contaminated. Wordlessly, he pointed fingers at the box, eyes bulging at the sacrilege committed and sinking deeper into his seat in discomfort at the horror of it all. If it had held dismembered dead bodies, he would not have been more horrified.

Murphy felt sorry for the pained expression that seemed to confirm Mr. O'Connor's world had been horrendously violated. He barely resisted the impulse to burst out laughing, throw his arms around this sad man, tell him they'd all be dead for years and suggest they go to the pub for a few pints and a bit of craic. Surely it would do him the world of good. Instead he frowned with what he hoped was a suitable degree of solemnity, tried to adopt a funereal tone, shook his head, and suggested that, perhaps, his filing competence was not all it should be. Mr. O'Conner, whose face was now fluctuating between purple and chalk white in dangerously rapid succession, opened a drawer and put pills into his mouth that he downed without water. This prompted a quick recovery and the launching of a sermon of fiery discourse about the importance of a well-organized filing system and the need to be better organized if Murphy was to become a successful insurance clerk. A disinterested Murphy heard little of the sermon but realized in fairness to the company and the public, he should no longer continue in that line of business.

Silence brought him back from his reverie. Apparently,

the lecture was over and a response was expected. Murphy offered his resignation, effective immediately. Mr. O'Connor barely succeeded in restraining himself from jumping over his desk and heartily clapping Murphy on the back. Both were relieved but the gloss soon wore off as Murphy wondered how to best tell his parents.

Only the year before, Murphy had wanted to emigrate to Australia on a special twenty-pound fare and had been approved to move there by the Australian government. Unfortunately, his parents had refused to allow him to live on the other side of the world. This time he found an alternative option a few days after his resignation while reading the Limerick Leader in the pub. "Apprentice fishermen needed. Enjoy the outdoors life as a trawler man. Earn big money. Be your own boss." Initially luke-warm to the prospect, he began to warm to it after a few more pints. Appealing images of him lying in the back of his big trawler sipping gin and tonics while vast quantities of fish leaped onto the deck decided him.

Three days later he met men from the Department of Fisheries who extolled the joys of a life on the ocean waves while also mentioning the Irish Navy was the only one that allowed its crew to go home for lunch each day. He signed paperwork that would have him training for seven months at a government school in Moville, County Donegal. That would be followed by five more months on an Irish trawler. Then he'd make the big money.

The morning he left his mother cried her heart out. As she stood with head bowed, sobbing uncontrollably, he wanted to reach out and console her but couldn't. That simply was not done. Instead he mumbled some inanity before walking away from her life.

He dropped in to the factory to say goodbye to his father.

"So, you're off."

"Aye."

"Call if you need anything. Good luck."

"Right. Bye now."

As he was walking out his father handed him an envelope then stood silently watching, hands clasped behind his back as his youngest child left. Driving away, Murphy saw his father still standing at the window watching him.

Driving through the town he felt elated. Free at last! He let out a mighty roar. People looked at him wondering who the madman was, while the few that recognized him simply rolled their eyes to heaven. Having been no farther north than Galway, he had no idea which would be the best route to Donegal, so he drove first to Galway then on to country Sligo where he intended sleeping for the night. Ben Bulban and Yeats's county spread out before him. He checked into a bed and breakfast in Sligo town that was fortunately over a pub.

Remembering the envelope, he opened it hoping it would contain some money. And it did, but there was also a hand-written note from his father.

"May the road rise up before you

May the wind always be at your back

May the sun shine warmly on your fields

But most of all, until we meet again

May God hold you safely in the palms of his hands."

Murphy's early euphoria disappeared like morning dew and was replaced by tears. He read the lines again and recognized what they wordlessly said. This was a declaration of love from his father who had never previously expressed any feeling of affection for his son.

Murphy headed for the bar and went on a tear that lasted deep into the night.

Chapter Twenty

MOVILLE

Minutes later, blinding light rudely forced itself through the curtains. Temporary relief came from a piercingly hot, then cold, shower followed by a deep gulp of gin for breakfast.

He headed out the road intending to be in Moville before nightfall. Apart from the lilt in people's accents, little changed until he was well north and crossed into Donegal. Now the transformation was dramatic. The land became forbiddingly rugged, angry, with black clouds floating above the towering mountain ranges.

Early winter snow had shrouded the region with lonely whiteness. Murphy traveled for over an hour without seeing any sign of life. The sense of isolation frightened him. He was alone in the world. His home in Limerick suddenly became appealing.

Finally, he turned a bend and his fear disappeared as he saw in the valley below smoke rising from cottages, and the makings of a village. His adventure resumed its rosy glow. More villages were passed until he came to a final hill. Below, his new home silently awaited him; a small town, more of a village, with a vast square at its center and the inevitable church spire dominating from the high ground. To the right the land sloped sharply downward to greet the waters of Loch Foyle. Murphy smiled, put the car into neutral, and silently glided down into Moville.

After parking in the square, he wondered what to do. He had a letter from the Department of Fisheries telling him to report to a Mr. Keavney who oversaw the school. He also had the address of the house where he would be staying. But that could all wait until later! Exhilarated at arriving and finally free from parents watching his every move, he briskly walked down a side street and looked out over Loch Foyle. Three ships plodded their way over the glassy surface, heading up to Derry.

Looking around he was pleased to see no shortage of pubs. When he walked into one that was practically empty all conversation between three old men immediately died. Instead they sullenly looked into the turf fireplace while furtively watching the stranger from beneath the shadow of their caps.

"Dia   duith."   Mumbled   the   bartender unenthusiastically.

"Dia duit agus Padraigh." Murphy responded.

Hearing the accent plus looking out and seeing the car registration plates, the bartender observed Murphy must have travelled some distance.

"I'm here for the fisheries school."

"Ah, tis dat time agin, Jimmy." This from one of the old men who inhaled deeply from his cigarette, farted loudly, then spat a bucketful of snot into the fire. After an eternity of awkwardness, the room began to defrost. Two of the men had spent a lifetime of ships, first in the Royal Navy during wartime then travelling the world with the Merchant Marine.

A few drinks later their faces beamed, fueled by memories of wild times they'd had in Shanghai, Taipei, Christchurch, Montevideo, and other exotic places Murphy had only seen on maps. The magic of their embellished tales carried him away. Soon a rake of empty frothy glasses cluttered the table. Dark now outside, realizing the time that was in it, Murphy shook hands with his new friends and reluctantly took his leave.

The place where he was to stay was just around the

corner so he knocked on the door of a sturdy looking stone house, similar to all the others that lined each side of the square. A scrawny old woman in blue overalls opened the door. Traces of while flower covered her blue apron. She had a bewildered look and silently stared at Murphy.

"Were you baking a cake for me?" He smiled with what he thought was consummate charm.

Her nostrils sniffed the Guinness from Murphy, her eyes narrowed and she glared disapprovingly. "Yer not allowed drink. Dadn't Master Keavney tell ye?"

And Murphy thought he'd left home. Chastened, he explained he'd only arrived an hour before and hadn't had time to meet Master Keavney.

"Ye got hare, man dear, over fure hours past. Bring yer gear in and meet da woman of de huse."

He went to his car and quickly rubbed toothpaste over his gums. The landlady turned out to be a big, warm woman who smiled a broad welcome that couldn't be overshadowed by the glowering witch hovering darkly behind her.

"Welcome, welcome! I'm Mrs. McAllister an ye've already met Agnes. She helps me round the huse. There'll be three other lads stain here witt ye. Arrivin tomorra.

Murphy nodded and smiled politely.

"Agnes'll show yer room."

Agnes' angry glare disappeared when Mrs. McAllister turned to her. Instead she smiled benevolently at Murphy as if they were the best of friends. "Aye, man dear, come on wit ye up."

The stairs wound up then around into a large room with three beds in it. Agnes opened another door that had a small room which was dominated by an enormous painting of an anguished looking Jesus Christ with a crown of nasty looking thorns on his head, his hand covering a bleeding heart. Agnes noticed Murphy's look of disgust which confirmed her already low opinion. "De ye hav a problem with dat lovely painting, man dear?"

"Not at all. It's the height of artistic excellence and esthetic ecstasy. I humbly tremble with anticipation in its divine presence."

After putting his clothes away, he went downstairs and told Mrs. McAllister he was going out for a while. He spent the remainder of the evening in the bar of a small hotel run by a man called Bill and his sister Eva. He would soon become friendly with them and occasionally mind the bar.

Several pints later Murphy rambled back to his lodgings, cautiously making minimal noise as he navigated the winding stairway. He began to wonder about his newfound liberty. Different warden, same bullshit.

Next morning, he woke shivering in a bitterly cold room. Barely washing because of the ice-cold water, he made his way downstairs. Breakfast was scalding hot tea strong as porter, bread with marmalade then more tea.

The time had come to meet the man who ran the school. It was in a dilapidated national school building hanging precariously high up a hill. The door groaned as he entered. Winds howling up from Loch Foyle blew with a vengeance making Murphy shiver. Pulling his coat tighter he called out "Hello, anyone here?"

A skeletal hand with well chewed nicotine stained fingers crawled out from behind the office door. The bent over body that followed was unhealthy and wizened. A keen intelligence lurked behind those hawkish eyes. A little man stood silently sniffing Murphy while taking a deep drag on his cigarette. A raspy voice said "Kem in. Ye got hare yastarday." He then turned his back on Murphy and beckoned with an emaciated arm.

Murphy had heard about Donegal people being tough but decent enough once they got to know you. He politely introduced himself then stood waiting.

"Ae want no trouble from ye lads this time, ye hare?"

Murphy wondered what damage previous groups had done. "I understand, Mr. Keavney. All I'm here for is to learn then I'll be off to the boats."

Mr. Keavney shifted from one foot to the other then spoke loudly "I'm not going te loose ma pension."

What the hell was he talking about? Murphy knew better than to respond.

"An no drinkin, goin inta pubs an getting girls pregnant."

"Mr. Keavney, I won't cause you any grief by getting a girl pregnant but I'm going to take the occasional pint. I'm nineteen.

Mr. Keavney's mind raced, wondering if his authority was being seriously challenged. "Well, yer the eldest boy on the course. Just don't give bad example te the younger lads ye hear me."

"Absolutely Mr. Keavney. I'll be the epitome of discretion."

He was then curtly dismissed and told to return in two days at nine sharp.

After returning to his lodgings, he was met on the staircase by a fuming Agnes protectively carrying a Jesus portrait under her arm.

"Ah don't know ye weren't one of us." She spat at Murphy as she pushed past him.

It was only after he went into his bedroom and noticed the blank space over his bed that he remembered; he'd arrived back from the pubs fairly on then angrily turned the Jesus painting around before passing out. After thirteen years of beatings from the Jesuits at school he wanted to never again be reminded about religion.

Agnes never forgave him. During the rest of his stay she'd angrily bang his plate down on the table while fawning over the other boys and giving them obviously larger portions to eat. Murphy further tormented her by constantly offering profuse thanks for every slight.

The three lads also staying at his house would arrive next day. Tony Davitt from western Mayo, Michael O Conlon from Spiddle, and Marcus Flynn from county Cork. Murphy took an instant liking to Tony and Michael and an equal dislike to Flynn.

Michael's family were all fishermen. He was born into, and for, the fisherman's life. Stocky in build with a rascally grim always about to spread over his freckled face.

Tony also came from a fishing family. He was dark in complexion like many Black Irish on the western coast, was incredibly shy, had crooked teeth that wandered in many directions, and was incapable of looking directly at anyone without blushing beet red.

Flynn was an insignificant streak of misery.

Next morning the four of them trooped up the hill for the first day of class. Thirty boys sat in the wind-swept classroom trying to unobtrusively observe each other.

The Hunchback limped in and glared angrily at his new charges. His opening remarks were accompanied by fierce wagging of his emaciated fingers as he confirmed his determination not to lose his pension. The reference was lost on all but Murphy who barely managed to suppress laughter.

The vulgar thread of intimidation that was integral to the Irish educational system was evident even in that classroom. Murphy had naively imagined the days of humiliation and degradation at the Jesuit school were well behind him but here was another taste of mental flagration as Mr. Keavney rained threats of hell and damnation on the useless hooligans he'd been burdened with. Several of the hooligans looked out the window wishing they were out on the sea rather than being imprisoned in a stuffy classroom with a demented dictator.

The lads quickly got to know each other. Apart from

a few misfits like Murphy, the other students came from fishing ports and were always destined for a life at sea. The average age was seventeen with the youngest fifteen.

The pecking order was quickly established. Murphy was extremely fit and the eldest, so nobody messed with him. Wee Tony Davitt was not so fortunate. During the first classroom break, Jerry Byrne, a Dublin gurrier, picked a cowardly fight with the diminutive Tony who, within seconds was on the ground getting his lights punched out.

Murphy jumped in and dragged Byrne away. "You'll leave him alone."

"Stay out a this." Spat Byrne, his face dark with rage.

"You'll leave him alone. You have an argument with him, you have one with me." This spoken in a calm but authoritative tone.

Byrne paused then wisely stepped back. "He bitter watch out, is all."

Murphy brought the bloodied but relieved Tony to the bathroom and helped clean the blood from his face and shirt.

His intervention earned him the begrudging respect of the other lads.

The long days turned into weeks then slowly into months during which they learned about navigation, overall seamanship, net mending, carpentry, cooking, sewing and even how to darn socks. It bore little resemblance to what Murphy had expected. He wasn't alone in that. Within a month, six of the lads had left. When the course ended five months later, only eighteen remained. A year later two were dead from drowning.

Chapter Twenty-One

THE BORROWED BUS

The Moville chapter of his life was quickly drawing to a close. A party was decided on two days prior to departure. Since most were in their mid-teens they weren't officially allowed to drink, but everyone did, so the party started early with everyone except Murphy getting langerzed as the night progressed. The usual local girls attached themselves to the group and paired off as inhibitions floated away the faster the alcohol flowed. As usual, Murphy remained alone.

Midnight came and they found themselves roaming the square looking for something to do. Murphy's gaze fell on a parked double decker bus. Without thinking he found himself opening the driver's side door. It was unlocked so in he climbed. There was no ignition key but when he pushed a black button the ancient bus shuddered then exploded into life. Another switch magically opened the side doors; then everyone laughingly charged in with the remaining crates of beer and whiskey bottles.

The thunderous sound of the engine reverberated around the empty square. Lights were turned on in some of the houses. Conscious of the unwanted attention, Murphy quickly gunned the accelerator and sputtered out of the square and up the road for Carandonagh. Having never driven anything bigger than a small car, the sudden upgrade was an interesting challenge but despite several close visits to the ditch he somehow managed to keep the bus on the road.

The sense of craic was mighty! The old bus shuddered

with the manic screams from teenagers delighted with their unexpected adventure. Harry Neilsen sang "I'm goin where the sun keeps shinin through the pourin rain. Goin where the weather suits my booooecennss. Skippin over the ocean breeze..."

Murphy drank deeper from his whiskey bottle while detachedly observing in the mirror his band of revelers as they laughed, kissed, and fondled, some innocently, others with total abandon. They unconsciously knew this adventure was ending. They probably would never meet again.

"Where we headin'?" one of the lads shouted while struggling with a bra strap.

"Haven't a clue."

A short time later the darkness was broken by the appearance of a watery moon which peeked through clouds, intermittently painting a roiling, angry sea with swathes of silver. Carandonagh beach! Murphy recognized the broad and endless length of it. Shortly after arriving in Moville, he had discovered this glorious beach and often went there alone, grateful for the isolated privacy its emptiness gifted him. He'd walk across the white sand, pausing momentarily at the water's edge before stripping off his clothes and plunging naked into the ice cold Atlantic. There, solitary in the universe, he'd powerfully swim through series of white capped waves until his body numbed. Then he'd reluctantly head for shore to emerge shivering but exhilarated, every atom in his body rejoicing with the innocence of unknown future pain. Still naked, he'd run at a furious pace along the shore, laughing and waving to the floating gulls, who, recognizing him, screamed salutations only kindred spirits exchange. He felt exhilaration from the yielding grains of sand shifting under his feet and the sound of the pounding surf which elevated him to become an integral part of its perfect unity. Emotions overwhelmed him when, beyond exhaustion, he knelt with arms outstretched, weeping uncontrollably because of the sense of awe experienced in his fleeting unity with the unseen.

But this night was loudly different. He parked the bus on the beach and flung the doors wide. Everyone merrily bounded off with whatever refreshment was left. Driftwood was gathered and a fire started using newspaper and petrol sucked from the bus. Soon a great blaze crackled and roared into the sparkling night sky. Boys and girls linked arms and danced around it in pagan abandon before collapsing, laughing onto the sand. Most disappeared into the dunes and created a few unwanted babies who would never know their fathers, while a few unpretty ones sat alone, untouched, same as past and future.

Emerging from the shadows, Murphy emptied the last of his whiskey bottle, wrote a message in it, then walked toward the shore and threw it into the embrace of the grasping breakers. He then walked back to the bus, climbed into the driver's seat, and started the engine. Despite protestations, everybody straggled over, and pulled and pushed each other inside. The doors were shut, and after great revving, they went roaring along the beach. Soon the wild Atlantic water splashed against the sides and everybody whooped and hollered as bus and waves collided, spewing spray up against the windows.

A foreboding whirring sound arose. Cheers turned to groans. Rear wheels spun wildly, screaming indignation as they became buried in wet, frothy sand.

"Get out and push the lot of you!" Murphy shouted over the tumult.

For all their heaving and shoving the wheels only sank deeper and deeper until they had to finally admit defeat and abandon ship.

Twenty previously joyous revelers turned glum as, soaked, cold and tired, they contemplated the tiresome eleven mile walk back to Moville. As they left Murphy stole a quick look back at the beach and cringed as he noticed the tide was coming in, not going out. With heart sinking as fast as the bus, he realized that, within a few hours, seawater would cover Moville's sole form of public transportation.

Spirits turned ugly. Murphy felt a collective anger turned against him as the weary group trudged their way silently homeward. When the solemn, raggedy bunch finally straggled into town they made their ways to respective lodgings in absolute quietness.

Alone in his room drunken remorse prevented Murphy from sleeping. He finally decided that the least he could do was let the police know where the bus was. He crept back downstairs then walked quietly over to the public phone box. The guard on night duty awoke from a deep slumber that quickly dropped away from him as he listened to Murphy explain, in the closest he could get to a Donegal accent, that the village bus had last been seen on Carandonagh beach and, what with the tide coming in, they might want to check it out. Conscience assuaged he went back up to bed and immediately sank into an exhausted slumber.

Moments later he was being shaken and voices reverberated against his eardrums. "Come-on, ye bollix, ye're comin' te the station."

Totally confused, Murphy's bleary eyes partially focused on two large men in blue uniforms. He'd drunk with them on occasion and served them after hours in Bill and Eva's hotel where he'd spent many evenings following the failure of one of his rare romantic endeavors. Now though, on this ridiculously early morning, there was no sense of frivolity or camaraderie. The effects of the drink were still on him and he was annoyed about being dragged from an interrupted sleep.

Sitting in front of a fuming Sergeant Boyle he furiously tried to think of a way out of his predicament. He wondered had they rescued the bus in time or had it become another victim of that violent sea? But he daren't ask. Perhaps he was in the process of becoming part of the local folklore. Sergeant Boyle smiled with cold eyes intended to penetrate Murphy's youthful arrogance.

"Ye lads always bring us trouble. Every year 'tis the same. Fights, drunkenness, though most of ye aren't old enough to drink; and babies, always a few bastards left for young girls to raise alone. I've asked the Department of Fisheries many times to move the school somewhere else, but no, it stays here. Over the years, I've come across almost every situation imaginable." At this he threw his arms wide as if addressing a large gathering. "But this, stealing a valuable bus then willfully and maliciously destroyin it…" He shook his head sadly, then asked in too quiet a voice "Why'd ye do it?"

Oh, Mother of Jesus, the bus was gone! The previous year's incident had been bad enough when his father had to write a check for a new car. What would a double decker bus cost? His parents would kill him when they heard about it!

But what did the Sergeant really know? "Why did I do what?" Murphy asked far more calmly than he felt.

"Don't get smart with me, my boy." Any pretense of civility was gone. "You're the only one of that crowd who has a car, or even a driver's license. You were seen, by a woman who lives across the square, getting into the bus, and driving out the Carandonagh road. Do ye deny it?"

Bluffing was all he could do. "She must have been mistaken, Sergeant. I went home right after the party. I admit I'd had a fair rake of pints and wouldn't have been in any condition to drive my own car, let alone a bus. Anyway, how could I start it? I'd need a key."

A sly look of recognition came over the Sergeant. The game was on. He looked across at one of his guards. "Well, Tommy, we've a rare schmart Alec here."

After being up half the night and trying to rescue the

bus, Tommy was exhausted, ill-tempered and would have liked nothing better than to have a few minutes in private with Murphy.

"Maybe Tommy should take you by himself into the cell fer a wee bit of a chat. It was he who got the call in the wee hours and had to drive out to Carandonagh to find the bus you stole. Poor man's hardly slept in the past day and gets very grumpy without sleep, don't ye, Tommy?

Tommy leaned forward veins bulging and eyes about to explode, a wild dog barely restrained on his leash and ready to draw blood and eat raw flesh. The room grew smaller and darker by the second.

"Sergeant, could I talk privately with you, please?"

Recognizing a breakthrough, and believing Murphy had come to his senses from fear or simply exhaustion, the Sergeant nodded to his men who reluctantly left. The brief respite allowed Murphy time to think.

Desperate times made for desperate measures. Sergeant Boyle sat patiently, smiling benignly, all traces of animosity gone. When they were alone he pushed a pencil and paper toward Murphy. "Just write down what ye did and we'll clear it all up."

Murphy's mind churned. His father had visited him a month ago. His Mercedes had been broken into and he'd had a conversation with the Sergeant. Murphy also knew they were chancing their arm about some resident of Moville seeing him. At the time, he'd borrowed the bus every soul in the village had already been snoring for hours. Even if one had claimed to see him, where was the legal proof? None of the lads would inform on him, except that bollix Marcus Flynn, who was annoyed Murphy had come in first overall in the school exams ahead of him. He was thick enough to grass on Murphy but he'd beat the bejazzus out of him as a warning.

"Sergeant, we both know there's no proof I did

anything. How could there be since I was in bed whenever whatever happened?" Murphy opened his arms wide, protesting his innocence.

The Sergeant's mustache began twitching overtime. His fingers drummed on his desk and he half rose as though to reach across before briefly hesitating.

"Sergeant, please don't take this the wrong way. I don't intend to be rude but you're but a year away from honorable retirement. Why would you want to bring problems on yourself after the distinguished career you've had?"

A look of confusion came over the man's face as he probably wondered what Murphy was talking about. But Murphy had learned the Sargent had been stuck in that remote outpost for the past twenty years having repeatedly been passed over for promotion by men far less qualified and junior to him. Adding insult to injury, Murphy had heard his father before him had been a proven patriot in the war for independence against the British but taken the wrong side in the civil war. His error had followed his family who were still being silently punished up to the present time.

Sensing an advantage, Murphy quickly continued, "Ye know Sargent, Sean Lemass is a good friend of our family. He's on the board of my father's company. Very imposing man." A pause while that sank in. Murphy began to take perverse pleasure at the sergeant's obvious discomfort. "And Dennis O'Malley, the Minister for Justice lives close by. Our families have known each other for years. I was in school with his son for a long time."

Silence, apart from the clock ticking. Both knew what was being unspoken. The Sergeant looked hard at Murphy. He thought about the recent well-publicized article in the national papers when a misfortunate Guard, just out of training and full of piss and vinegar, had raided a pub in Limerick that was serving drinks after hours. One of the customers was the Honorable Minister for Justice, Murphy's family friend Dennis O'Malley, another Crescent boy. When he invited the policeman to sit down and have a drink the fool had primly and extremely naively quoted the drinking hours' law, chapter, and verse to the well-on gathering.

"Now let me tell you an unwritten law," the minister had responded. "It gets very lonely and cold out on Valentia Island chasing shadows, so why don't ye take yer ease and join us?"

Inexplicably the idiot guard had refused and insisted on issuing a summons to the minister and his cronies. Within twenty-four hours he was viewing the distant mainland from Valentia Island.

Instead of the news causing a problem for the minister his stock rose as few people had sympathy for the young, idiot guard. The Sergeant turned the story over in his mind. Disgusted with himself but resigned to life's constant cruelty, he suddenly broke into a big smile and started to laugh, "You know what; we were able to get the bus out with two tractors before the tide came in too far. There's some sand stuck in the wheels but they'll clear that easily enough. Sure, I was young myself once and have stories I couldn't tell you."

They were both laughing their heads off like long lost friends when the two guards came back in with puzzled expressions frozen on their faces. Murphy shook hands with the Sergeant, excused himself, left the room and went home. Quickly he packed without saying goodbye to anyone, then immediately headed out the road and sped away from Moville as fast as his old Vauxhall Velox could go.

Inexplicably, instead of heading to the safety of the south, with an impulsive decision he'd soon regret, he found himself driving towards Derry to see what all the fuss was about.

Chapter Twenty-Two

DERRY

"Where ye goin'?" the morose border guard at Muff asked as he casually picked his teeth without taking his cold eyes off me.

"Derry or Londonderry," Murphy responded cheerfully.

"Londonderry is what the bastards call it."

Murphy had just been introduced the bitterness of Northern Ireland politics. Muff was the border post on the Irish Republic side ten miles up from Moville. He was now entering the six counties of Ireland which were still under British control. Although he'd read about the horror stories of Catholics being burned out of their homes and being attacked by the Protestant B Specials, the police force, until now it had all been theoretical. Like most people in the Irish Republic, he had limited concern about it. The British government had brought in an army that had initially been welcomed by the Catholic community as they patrolled their ghettos.

The patrol guard snapped his toothpick in half and flicked it onto the hood of Murphy's car, checked the registration and begrudgingly threw a docket, telling Murphy to take it to a British army post called the White House once he arrived in Derry. The guard's icy winter stare made Murphy happy to be on his way.

The drive would take half an hour. Murphy was eager to see the city he'd read so much about in his history books. Derry was where the battle of the Boyne, among the most significant in Irish history, had been fought creating tragic consequences that endured up to the present day.

After arriving in the center of Derry he went for lunch then walked around the Diamond area. Despite occasional laughter a palpable tension pervaded the atmosphere. Murphy was startled to see heavily armed soldiers everywhere, many of them nervous, pimply young lads with frightened eyes. Saracen APCs were everywhere. At several intersections tanks sat, engines warm and ready to roar. Outside Woolworth's soldiers carefully searched him and everyone else coming and going from that busy store. Murphy had sufficient sense not to say anything and reveal his southern accent. What hell had he walked into just a few miles away from quiet Moville? He would soon get a harsh response to that question.

Being unfamiliar with Derry and having lunch, plus some shopping to do, it was over three hours before he finally made his way to the entrance of the appropriately named White House, a dour, uninteresting building, all white. British soldiers stood outside with weapons at the ready. Murphy was about to joke with them about their weapons having little resemblance to the pitiful 303s he'd had in the Irish army but their expressionless eyes advised otherwise.

A fraction of a second after he presented his papers all hell broke loose. "He's here!" roared the Sergeant from behind the desk. With that two soldiers grabbed Murphy, bent his arms behind his back and dragged him across the floor. Moments later he was thrown into a dark cell. What in hell had he done? He sat on the floor bewildered, frightened. Soon he would be terrified. Occasionally a small hatch opened then quickly closed and eyes looked in at him. An eternity later three soldiers, one tall officer with a strange, sunken face, a sergeant and two privates, entered. "Stand up," the officer ordered, much too loudly for the small room. Murphy struggled to get to his feet but was stiff and slow. He'd almost made it when the officer belted him across the face, then slammed him against the wall. "Lazy, fucking paddy, I don't have all day!" He towered over Murphy, screaming in a high-pitched, effeminate voice that singed Murphy's ears. He squeezed his eyes shut as the officer raised his baton. His right arm exploded and Murphy screamed with pain as bones shattered. He fell banging his head on the concrete floor, frantically trying to understand why all this was happening. The only sound was someone whimpering and it took a moment before he realized who it was. Someone struck a match. "All right, men," the sergeant said. Murphy looked up to see two soldiers, like grinning baboons, moving purposefully toward him. He cowered back against the wall, expecting the worst. All he could remember afterward was the shine of their polished boots as they repeatedly kicked his body while carefully avoiding his face. Pain screamed internally as the pounding continued and bones were broken and internal bleeding began. Mercifully, he finally fell unconscious.

He was blind and wet after being shook awake. They'd put a hood over his head and dumped a bucket of iced water over him. Dragging him to a standing position they began to push him from one to another. It became a game where one would catch him, then another – then no one would so he'd crash to the concrete floor. That's when they laughed the hardest and shrillest, like inmates of a lunatic asylum. The officer, in an increasingly impatient voice, urged Murphy to tell them who he'd seen in the Bogside. They threw out names he'd never heard of and wouldn't believe him when he gasped that he has no idea where the Bogside was, this was his first time ever being in Derry. "It's Londonderry, you Fenian bastard" He pitifully cried out they must have confused him with someone else. This made them angrier and increased the level of violence. Disoriented and dizzy his head exploded while his body convulsed until the pain was so powerful he again lost consciousness.

Later when he woke, he was alone in the cell. All sense of time was gone. Tears of loneliness poured down his battered face. Completely disorientated, he saw his father's smiling face and longed to run toward him and be lifted into those strong, comforting arms. His mother then appeared, floating over the gentle fields of his childhood, a place overflowing with swaying yellow daffodils, purple bluebells, and red roses. She was smiling from an unlined, serene face and outstretched arms invited him to the safety or comfort of her love.

That's when they brought in the dogs. There were two, possibly three. "Some hungry German Shepherds here to play with you," an unfamiliar voice said. They were inches from Murphy's face and barking excitedly. Frozen with terror he stopped breathing. Then he wet himself and when shit ran uncontrollably he began sobbing hysterically. The canine handlers found this hilarious. Their laughter contrasted with the violent snarling of their dogs.

Time disappeared. Next thing he felt was his head being gently held and a cup of water put to his bleeding lips.

"It's all right lad, take a sip." This from a soft lilting voice, perhaps a Donegal man. Murphy fearfully looked into gentle, sensitive eyes. They belonged to a small, old man in a dark rumpled suit. Ever so carefully he took Murphy's arm and slowly helped him get up then guided him over onto a chair that hadn't previously been there.

"I'm really sorry about all this. Those army lads are a rough bunch. All they understand is violence. No finesse, at all, at all. Unfortunately, the troubles here in Londonderry and Belfast have set them on edge." He shook his gray head and sighed at the absurdity of it all. Murphy wondered was he hallucinating, but no, the man seemed real. His body ached and he had serious trouble breathing. He coughed and pain screamed at him. "What have I done?" He whispered unevenly.

"That's what those thugs want to know. So, before they come back why don't ye just tell me and we'll have ye out of here in no time at all."

"Jesus Christ, all I did was drive around Derry for a while before coming to his hell hole!"

"It's Londonderry, lad. Why do ye call it Derry?" He said this in a soft, silky tone so gentle Murphy had to strain to hear. He couldn't think of an answer that would please so he remained silent. "Ye crossed over the border at ten to twelve this morning and were instructed to come here to the White House immediately upon arriving in Londonderry. Ye were supposed to present yer papers for inspection, but there was no sign of ye for over four hours. That's what has those lads worried. They think ye were over in the Bogside talking to some of yer Fenian friends."

His interrogator could not have possibly missed Murphy's look of astonishment. "I don't even know where the damned Bogside is." He'd read in the papers it was the Catholic Nationalist area of Derry but beyond that he knew little else. By then Murphy frantically realized he'd better convince the quiet man he posed no threat or he'd never get back across the border which was the only place he wanted to be. Nobody knew where he was. Clearly, they could do whatever they wanted with him and no one would be any the wiser if he disappeared entirely. "Look, I don't have any politics. I don't know or give a damn about what's happening up here. It's true." From the expressionless response Murphy couldn't tell if he was believed. "I've been attending the Irish government fisheries school in Moville. Just came here to look around then head back down south to work on a boat in Dingle."

The man began to ruffle through some papers. Stopping at one he read it to himself, muttering. He kept his finger on one item that seemed of interest. "You seem to be

a good rugger player. Did you enjoy playing in Cheshire?"
How the hell did he know that? It had been over a year since
he'd played in Hoylake when on an insurance course with
the Royal Insurance Group.

The man in the suit looked intently at Murphy for
an eternity. Murphy tried to stare back but lost all resolve
as the pain in his body returned. After prolonged silence, he
cleared his throat having come to a decision. "You do seem
a decent lad. I'm sure it was all a misunderstanding. Can't
promise anything but will have a chat and see what I can
do. But if you ever come back to Londonderry and happen
to visit the Bogside you will behave yourself, won't you?
There's a lot of hot headed IRA thugs in there. Wouldn't be
wise to get caught up with them; a nasty bunch."

In that moment Murphy would have sold his mother's
soul to the devil so he enthusiastically agreed not only to
behave himself, but never again to revisit the North.

Alone again, he wondered was it day or night? How
long had he been unconscious? He ached both inside and out.
Two teeth were gone and several lose, his lips had stopped
bleeding but several ribs were either broken or fractured, and
he still couldn't control his bowel movements.

Finally, the cell door opened and he sat waiting on
his fate. If those army bastards came back and worked him
over again he'd tell them anything they wanted to hear, agree
to all the names he did not know, and sign any statement
confirming his guilt about anything. It was the tall army
officer who came back. "Well now, everything seems to be in
order. You're free to leave." This said with a friendly smile,
chums clearing up a minor understanding. Then he turned
his back, nodded for Murphy to follow him. Walking was
difficult but he summoned up all his strength as he hobbled
out the door. His car had been turned inside out.

Twenty minutes later he arrived at the Muff border
post.

"Where are ye comin' from?" Asked the Irish guard looking at the Free State license plates.

"Derry," Murphy responded in a lifeless tone. "Or Londonderry, as the Bastards call it."

Chapter Twenty-Three

DINGLE

Standing at the top of O'Connor's Pass, Murphy patiently waited for dawn to break. "Red sky at night sailor's delight, Red sky at morning sailor's warning." Last night a darkly reddening sunset had flexed as with thick layers of blood. This morning however, even in near darkness, the color of the sky boded poorly for the fishermen who would, even then, be making their way out to the fishing grounds beyond the sanctuary of Dingle Bay, deeper towards the Schelligs and points beyond. The black cloak of nighttime was slowly pushed aside by wiggling shadows of light, which reached with authority through the gloom. To his right the valley below appeared as rich and magnificent as when he'd first seen it a few years previously. An energetic stream which began lazily high up in the mountains before gathering strength on its journey downward, chattered beside him.

The sun silently exploded high above a forest bent but not beaten by thousands of years of violent winds, and changed the plunging water into quivering golden lava vibrant on its journey down the valley. Looking westward to Dingle Bay, he wondered if the Morning Star, the fishing trawler he'd been assigned to, was among those boats now making her way out to the fishing grounds. He took the crumpled Department of Fishery's letter from his pocket. He was going to serve five months as an apprentice deck hand before he'd earn the right to the good money. At the age of twenty, that seemed a long time to wait. The letter fluttering in his hand told him to report to John Flannery, the Morning

Star skipper.

Above him, out of the shimmering mist, came a magnificent stag with massive antlers making his imperial way across his territory while giving Murphy a disinterested look before leisurely turning away. Then the bleating of the mountain sheep began, first one then another, building up to an unholy Greek chorus. T'was time to move on.

Not much was stirring in Dingle at seven o'clock on that or any other morning. The occasional chimney showed smoke rising lazily but, apart from that, not a soul stirred. A variety of dogs, some animated others seemingly dead, lounged on street corners and outside homes. Driving through the village he found himself at the pier where two trawlers, looking sad and weary, cringed against the quay, grumbling their woes. There was no sign of the Morning Star. Gulls were flying out to sea, screeching impatiently for their morning feed. Since the boats wouldn't be back till early evening, they headed out the peninsula towards Ballydavid. It had been seven years since he'd attended the Irish language summer course there with other boys from school. He laughed to think of the trouble he and some of the lads had gotten into. Now everyone had moved on with their lives, mostly to college in Dublin and Cork, while he was a trainee fisherman.

He drove back to Dingle and passed the remainder of the day walking about exploring its hilly winding streets, one tumbling upon the next like an untidy deck of cards. There were little shops that sold groceries, sewing, and knitting supplies, sweets, and other things necessary to the villagers. Inside, ancient women, many draped in black shawls, stared out from behind thick-rimmed spectacles. Fishy smells came from the occasional chipper and closer to the water were more shops filled with things only tourists would buy. They had only the few summer months to capture tourist trade before going on the dole for winter. And, like all small towns, Dingle had pubs beyond all proportion to the number of town inhabitants and had many thirsty throats to serve. Murphy's was another one.

The June sun was about to go to bed far out in the Atlantic when the first of the trawlers appeared around the Dingle headland. Shortly after, two more followed. A thrill of anticipation rushed through Murphy and, as they came towards the pier he saw the name Morning Star on the bow of a blue and white boat. It had obviously seen its share of trawling, yet retained a level of dignity as it turned inland, its decks low in the water, carrying what must have been a grand day's catch. Three men were on deck with another in the wheelhouse. Even at a distance one of the men seemed a giant, towering over the other two who appeared to be broad and stocky. When they arrived at the quay, he wondered should he wait until the next day to introduce himself. Suddenly a rope was hurled up at him and he was tying it to the bollard. "Go raibh milte maith agat," a rich, singing Kerry voice thanked him. It was the giant speaking.

Murphy silently watched while they unloaded their haul, a mixture of mackerel and white fish. He waited until they left the boat, and saw them head to Mikey Long's place which was the pub closest to the quay. Taking a deep breath, he followed them in.

"Is John Flannery one of you?" A small sized man with a deeply lined, brown face slowly looked up from his pint, foam forming an uneven stripe along his upper lip. Murphy wondered if he'd seen him before.

"Who is it wants him?" his quiet voice asked. Then Murphy remembered. "I saw you on television. About the Irish fishing industry, it was. You talked about the problems of the Dingle fishermen. I'm Murphy, your new deckhand," he breathlessly blurted out, then felt somewhat ridiculous as he handed his skipper the letter from the Department of Fisheries. Murphy stood as tall as his five feet nine inches allowed, stuck his chest out, and broadened his shoulders in a vain attempt to measure up to the hardened fishermen who were casting dubious, sideways glances.

"Welcome. I'm John Flannery." Then he just remained standing, said nothing. Neither did anybody else. Murphy wondered if they were always like this or simply collectively disgusted with the miserable specimen of trawler man the Department of Fisheries was producing. The giant now moved towards him towering, glared down, and burst out with an unnatural laugh that shook the room and extended a hand nearly as big as Murphy's arm. Then he thundered in a voice rich with Kerry dialect, "De ye knooww who I am?" How could Murphy know? Shaking his head sadly at Murphy's ignorance, the giant continued with evident pride, "I'm the Great Paddy Bawn Brosnan." Then he shook his head and repeatedly blinked his eyes, waiting for a response. Murphy's new crewmates looked on eagerly, enjoying his discomfort. Out of desperation Murphy reasoned that, since the county of Kerry had historically been a powerhouse in Gaelic football, and with Paddy Bawn being such an enormous man, perhaps he'd been a Kerry footballer. With nothing to lose he stammered, "I do know you. You're a famous Kerry footballer!" The great Paddy Bawn turned around, laughing triumphantly, "Ya see lads, I'm famos avrywhare."

While drinking a few pints of Guinness, Murphy began to learn more about the other crewmembers. Both the men, Peadar and Liam, were from the Dingle peninsula, both married and one of them happily so. He soon found out that Peader was ambitious, wanted to have his own boat in which to travel over to Dunmore East and further for the lucrative herring season. Liam, trapped in a miserable marriage, didn't seem to care much about anything except getting by. Paddy Bawn was by far the liveliest and most content. Apart from being famous in the county and beyond, he had a pub in the main street, which provided a steady income, so he fished on the boats mainly because of his love of the sea and a need to channel his still enormous energy.

John Flannery was an entirely different matter altogether. Immediately on meeting him, Murphy sensed a profound sadness masked by classically Irish stoicism. It only took a few days before he learned John's wife had scarpered with all the money they'd had in the bank; saved from the fishing and a small shop they owned. And to add insult to injury, she'd also taken a local lad with her for company to points unknown, leaving John to be laughed at while raising, by himself, their only child, a dark- haired beauty. Shortly after Murphy's arrival his daughter disappeared overnight. She called John a month later to say she was in London and not coming back. Through it all John displayed no emotion, nor did he ever discuss any part of his personal life. Murphy soon came to realize that the weather-beaten face and world weary eyes he'd viewed during our first meeting rarely changed and, in fact, represented John's perpetually worldview. This world-weary man was incapable of feeling any more pain.

Murphy asked where he'd be living, as the Department said he was supposed to receive lodging. John paused before looking out the window of Mikey Long's pub, then pointed silently to the Morning Star. "Four berts dare. Take yer pick. We'll be settin' out round five in the morn." Murphy walked unsteadily down the quay to his new home, climbed onto the deck, went below, selected a bunk bed, and quickly fell into a deep sleep.

Moments later he was abruptly shaken awake by Paddy Bawn who seemed even larger than the night before. Sickening diesel fumes poured from an engine located a few yards from where Murphy had slept. Quickly he stumbled onto his feet and climbed up to the deck. It was still dark and the clock had barely turned five. Mother of God what an unearthly hour to be awake! His new colleagues were already busy examining nets and sorting lines. Murphy stood anxiously awaiting instructions, unsure of what his task should be. The skipper, above in the wheelhouse, looked down giving a barely perceptible nod of recognition. Peader and Liam paused in their work to greet him, then away the Morning Star moved from the quay.

Nervous but excited anticipation rushed through Murphy as they left Dingle behind. The occasional house light blinked farewell as dawn began to wake and the open sea beckoned them onward toward the fishing grounds. All the time and effort spent at the Fisheries school was about to come to fruition! He was on his way to fulfilling the next part of his long-term plan. Within five years he intended to have three boats of his own fishing the west, south, and east coasts. He had planned all this during his Moville winter but now, with the sea all around him, it was becoming real. His boats would provide fresh supplies to his fish and chippers and to the wholesale fish shops. He might also open a processing plant. He would be as successful as his father, perhaps more so. His parents would be proud of him yet.

"Strip the schnoods!" the voice of the skipper interrupted Murphy's daydream. What the hell was he talking about? Skipper pointed to the stern of the boat where lobster pots were piled six deep. Realizing their new man hadn't a clue what was expected of him, Skipper signaled to Paddy Bawn to advise him. "Dare's old bait in dem pots. Untie dem an tie fish bate on."

Climbing over the pots Murphy realized that one slight mistake in balance would be the end of him. The sea was rough and unforgiving. He'd already heard that, gentle Tony Davit from county Mayo, a boy he'd saved from being bullied in Moville, had drowned. A horrible death it must have been Tony, being dragged slowly down, your waders and lungs quickly filling with salty seawater, your last sight perhaps being the Mayo coastline and the stern of the disappearing boat. Then your terrified face, arms, then hands, must have disappeared. Making matters sadder, his body was never found for a decent burial, leaving his soul condemned forever to wander uneasily in the deep Atlantic darkness. Murphy shuddered and set his mind to surviving.

After he'd stripped the old bait he threw the lobster pots up towards where Liam had cut up fish saved from the previous day's catch. He placed bait inside each pot, which had a net at the entrance that would trap the lobster after it had entered. Then Peadar tossed each pot splashing into the ocean, at intervals of a hundred yards apart, where they quickly floated into the deep. Red buoys marked each one 'til the next day when they'd return to check. Then they were away again.

A small island appeared with hundreds of rabbits happily dancing over it. Murphy laughed and pointed them out to the lads. Looks of terror spread over their faces as they deliberately turned away from the merry sight. Now what had he done wrong? After a minute's silence, Paddy Bawn came to tower over him and shake a mighty finger in Murphy's face. "Never, never talk bout dose animals." Murphy knew better than to ask why. The other lads glared menacingly at him and, between their looks and Paddy Bawn's sincerity, he was convinced never to mention rabbits again. He found out later that it was an old superstition and considered bad luck to talk as he had, a forewarning of the imminent sinking of the boat. Such fear among the crew was probably magnified by the fact that none of them could swim because that might tempt fate. Knowing they had neither life jackets nor a dingy wouldn't help matters.

As they made their way closer to the fishing grounds the sense of isolation he always felt after losing sight of land settled on Murphy. The sky had become cloudy; no blue anywhere. The ocean churned up angry white caps as if forming some uncertain mood. Soon a vast whiteness stretching to the horizon. Murphy felt part of a landscape painting. Lines from Coleridge's Rhyme of the Ancient Mariner ran through his head. He barely resisted checking the horizon for sight of an albatross. They were completely alone in the world.

It took another hour to reach deeper out where the first nets were cast. They trawled for a time before finally drawing the nets in. Where there had been no other life now, suddenly, the skies were full with screaming seagulls. Murphy wondered where they'd come from and how they knew how to perfectly time their arrival? He felt a rush of excitement as the net broke the surface with seawater sloshing in all directions. It was bulging thick. Then, without warning, the boat was attacked from above. Bombs missed the trawler, but only barely. They came fast, by the hundreds, causing great explosions of water where they landed.

Panicking, Murphy dove for whatever cover he could find while frantically looking toward the horizon to see where the barrage was coming from. Raucous, dismissive laughter greeted him from his crewmates as they observed his terror. Looking up to where they pointed he saw gannets in their hundreds diving at breakneck speed from high above. They must have been diving at a hundred miles an hour, their wings outstretched then, with astonishing skill and precision, closing them a fraction of a second before hitting the water. Embarrassed and humiliated Murphy stood up and nonchalantly shrugged his shoulders, while the laughter continued to follow, ringing loudly in his ears.

The net was hauled aboard, Peader opened it and soon they were knee deep in an assortment of sea life all wiggling frantically across the deck. Then the sorting began. Mackerel, whiting, sole, some sea bass, crabs, unwanted conger eels and dogfish, also some unusual, ugly species Murphy didn't recognize but didn't want to ask about and further confirm his ignorance.

The nets were thrown out again into the deep and they spent the next hour separating the fish into boxes full with ice. Come nighttime they'd unload them at the docks, hopefully receiving a decent price; if that time ever came, and Murphy was beginning to think it never would! His hands were in agony with the coldness of the wriggling creatures, and he wondered how long before his fingers fell off. Eventually they became numb and when the last fish was put away, and he looked, it was a relief to see, although bleeding, they were not further damaged.

Time for food. Paddy Bawn, apparently, was the cook. Murphy hoped he'd washed his hands after doing a shit over the side of the boat and wiping his arse with a page from the Kerryman newspaper. Murphy watched the giant grab a bunch of mackerel in his huge fists, make his way to the cabin and gut them. The smell of frying arose to make his mouth water.

As they sat below, eating the best meal Murphy had ever tasted, he asked how prices were set for the catch. "Tis all up te de middle man and what de demand is 'cause of oter catches," explained John.

"We're in competition with other boats and other ports?" Murphy wondered. "So, what happens if there's little demand and we arrive back at port loaded down with a great haul of fish?"

"Dat's de problim wit all o' dis. If dare's no demand we jus sell te intervention or to de factories dat make cat food."

Murphy sat drinking tea stronger than porter and wondering at the business inefficiency of fishing in Ireland. Each day all the boats would sail out early, well before dawn, fish all day, come back into port at night, then hope for the best about market prices. It all seemed a ridiculous way of operating a business. He'd already heard the Dutch boats were bigger and far better equipped with sonar and radar that allow them to quickly identify shoals of fish and even the type of fish. Also, as they had freezing facilities on board that allowed them to keep their catch in perfect condition, they could stay in the North Sea fishing for ten days at a time before returning to port.

When he mentioned having heard this and that the big Japanese, Russian, and Norwegian fleets had factory ships that did everything, including canning on board, Peader spat with disgust, "Yes and dere nets are miles wide. Dey take more in wan haul dan we'd take in a month of Sundays. The other crewmembers grunted and spat in affirmation.

Murphy wondered how they could compete against such odds and at the apparent inefficiency of a daily return to port with absolute uncertainty regarding the possible value of our catch. The prices paid were important to everyone except him, being the new deckie. Each member received a share of the sale price, with another share to the boat, and a couple of shares going to the skipper who also owned the boat. You could work your tail off on a fifteen-hour day; arrive back with a boatload of fish, only to find they were only worth a penny or less each. It all seemed bloody well stupid.

Yet day after day, out they went and, although Murphy generally liked the sea and the rough company of the men, most of the time he found himself bloody well miserable with cuts on his hands and great blisters that never seemed to harden even as time passed. His teeth were ready to fall out from the chattering they did. Sometimes he thought he'd never get warm again – or get enough sleep.

After three months of repeatedly proving to everyone but himself that he was an inept deckhand, he had an accident that proved to be the tipping point. They'd been trawling all day and taking in the final catch when the nets got fouled up. Using a crow bar as instructed, Murphy was leaning hard when he lost his balance and caught his arm in the winch. The same had happened to a former student at the fisheries school and he'd lost his arm. Murphy didn't want his nickname to be Stumpy. As he watched his hand move deeper into the machinery he screamed in horror and pain. Peader roared at the skipper, who, fortunately for Murphy, noticed his dilemma and turned off the power. They roughly disentangled his arm. Fortunately, only one finger was badly damaged. The middle finger of his left hand was cut in two and lay wide open like a gutted fish.

John disappeared into the cabin, returning with a brandy bottle, which he liberally poured over the gaping wound. You could have heard Murphy's screams back in Limerick as the alcohol burned into his bloody flesh and mangled bones. John then wrapped the finger in cloth, glared at Murphy and walked away as Murphy sheepishly looked around expecting some level of sympathy. None was forthcoming. Apparently, his gruesome experience impressed no one. In fact, they were clearly annoyed, perhaps frustrated by the inconvenience of the extra workload they now faced.

Murphy never went for medical attention and, through the following weeks, he spent his time in local pubs while the finger slowly healed, although crookedly. The day before he was due to return to work, John took him into the parlor of his home. They sat in uncomfortable silence, while the skipper shuffled his feet back and forth on the faded green linoleum kitchen floor and looked trance like, at the dull gray ceiling. Finally, after a foghorn like clearing of his throat, he blurted out that the lads had decided Murphy would be better off taking his talents elsewhere.

Murphy looked blankly while the words slowly registered in his brain. When he finally realized that he'd been fired he was genuinely shocked. Anger and self-righteous indignation swelled up inside him. How dare they! Didn't these people know who he was? He glared silently at

John who furtively returned his stare before quickly turning away. Suddenly a fistful of fear exploded inside Murphy's gut and he let out a rush of air. Then he felt shame. There was John, as decent and noble a man as he'd ever likely to meet, who'd always treated him with the utmost of patience and civility, and Murphy was acting like a complete shite.

Then a flood of relief moved through his body. Apparently, it had been obvious to everybody except him that he wasn't cut out to be a trawler man. It had all been a naïve illusion. He considered the fire and accepted the new reality. He wondered how he could explain this to his parents. He could already hear his mother's "I told you so." spitting from between the cigarette smoke. Now what would he do with his life? Perhaps they'd allow him to immigrate to Australia. He walked over to John, shook his hand, and thanked him for the experience.

Murphy spent his final night in Dingle saying goodbye to all the pubs and getting drunk. The more he drank, the sadder he became. All his grandiose plans for a lucrative future in the fishing industry were gone. Even through the fogbank of alcohol, in those temporary moments of lucidity that it inspired, he could find nobody to blame except himself.

The following morning, despite a roaring hangover, he got up early and drove his car back up the mountain to O'Connor's Pass. Standing where he'd innocently stood a few months previously, he climbed onto the wall and was greeted with a clear view of the valley and the bay shimmering below. Impulsively he took off his cap, waved it in a circle above his head in salute, then turned his back on Dingle and on his brief fisherman's life.

Chapter Twenty-Four

A SON

The scowling nurse with life weary face, wobbly chins hiding a neck above a torso that sunk into an enormous arse and tree trunk legs, sniffed disapprovingly then waddled forward. "Ye can see her but only fer a minute."

Theresa lay exhausted. In the open ward were thirty other women, some still swollen, others having delivered. She was wasted on the drugs they'd given her. She urgently grasped Murphy's hand and dragged him to her with surprising strength. "Murph, I've given you a son." Then she sank into a deep sleep. Nurse Ratchet abruptly led him away. "Can I see my son?" "He's in the recovery room with the other newborns. Ye can look through the window. No disturbing him."

Murphy peered through the glass which was did little to muffle the squawking of babies who were clearly unhappy about departure from their mother's comfort. Ugly would be a charitable way to describe them. Crimson faces, clenched like wrinkled rashers and dribble oozing from their mouths, toothless and wizened. Their shriveled bodies squirmed and shook, some uncontrollably, but then he saw his son, beautifully shaped with an elegant mouth. He was calmer than the others and frowned at their outrageous shenanigans. Beaming with pride the new father energetically left the hospital to continue celebrations in a pub.

Murphy had been on the piss for at least a week before the baby was born. Before that, he'd been at home looking at his wife as she lay uncomfortably on the couch like a beached whale, huffing and puffing as she struggled in vain to position herself comfortably. She was nervous. "Hope the baby's all right. Are you really happy we're having it?" As if his opinion mattered. She'd gone from complaining she wasn't showing, to repeatedly commenting on how fat she'd become, then being revolted by the ugliness she saw in the mirror. Adding to his discomfort, she constantly peppered him with never ending questions, nagging about if he still loved her! Matters came to a head when he unwisely agreed with her that yes, indeed, she was huge. She was almost nine months pregnant, of course she was big! It's what happens when you are pregnant he explained. This resulted in an outpouring of screaming and tears while she told him what a shit he was to call her ugly. Bewildered as he always was by the perennial lack of female logic, he decided to go to the village for a pound of butter.

After a weeklong search, his brother in law finally tracked him down in a Blarney Street pub. He'd been on the piss for a week and sleeping in bed and breakfast houses while drinking his way across Cork city. Theresa was in the hospital about to have the baby while screaming obscenities about her bastard husband who finally reappeared a few hours after the birth.

There were complications and the baby had to stay in the hospital for two weeks. Finally holding him in his arms Murphy marveled at how fragile and small his son was. Surely defenseless to safely face the challenges waiting for him. He decided they'd call him Brian.

He regularly visited Theresa at the hospital where she stayed with the baby. On the day they were coming home, she begged Murphy to wait and leave with them. As he felt her tugging on his sleeve, with Brian gurgling at her breast, her demands rankled. "I must be off to clean up the house. Get everything ready for the both of you." With that, he abruptly left.

On the way home, resentment simmered. Was he now condemned to a life of endless servitude with this woman and child? Arriving at the country house outside Carrigaline, he noticed the place was a mess after his week alone. He'd pick up a bottle in the village, then get on with cleaning. But first had a quick drink at Rosie's bar and was about to leave when he met his friend Freddy Greene, who owned a bar over in Passage West. Freddy insisted they wet the baby's head. Not wanting to be rude, Murphy then bought a round. Then others joined in, one drink led to another until someone mentioned supper. Murphy looked at his watch horrified to observe it had suddenly become evening. He'd be in deep shit arriving home so late, and the house was still a mess!

On the drive home, he hoped in vain the release date had been postponed, but as he rounded the final bend, there was no escape - the house lights were all on. He heard Theresa crying before he opened the door. She was sitting on their bed, looking distraught, head in hands rocking back and forth keening like an old woman at a wake. "You bastard! You said you had to leave me to come home and clean up. Look at the place!" She dramatically pointed to the chaos, "Tis worse than a fucking pig sty!" "Little fellah looks good," he responded hoping to distract her as he looked at his heir in the cradle. This produced another avalanche of tears. "You don't give a damn, do you? All you care about is your bloody drink! What kind of father are you going to be? What kind of example for your son?" This was followed by a swishing of her hand toward Brian who now, awakened by the shouting, began to scream in harmony with his hysterical mother. Something in Murphy's head snapped and he stormed out while Theresa shouted, "Don't leave, please, damn you, please don't!" But he did. Fortunately, some of the lads were still in Rosie's when he returned and, quickly drowning a few whiskies, he silenced the angry voices in his head that condemned his behavior.

A few months later they had a formal celebration. Murphy's mother didn't attend but his father was in great form, dancing wildly with Theresa's sisters and making a great impression all round with his jokes and ability to make people feel good. Murphy felt proud of his father in a positive way he doubted his son would ever feel about him.

Brian was moved into a room of his own where he lustily cried during many a night. Theresa wanted to bring him into their bed for comfort but Murphy insisted he work it out on his own, and eventually he did.

Murphy found himself beginning to feel great affection for the little creature who was his son. Something indefinable stirred in his heart as he held him. He found himself increasingly going to the nursery door and just standing watching him. Initially he felt awkward when trying to play with Brian, having no reference point to know what to do as he had no memory of his parents ever playing with him or showing affection.

Time flew. Brian learned to crawl then to walk but Murphy saw few of these special moments because he'd became busy building the business. Theresa turned into one of those nagging wives he'd heard other lads complain about; always going on about his drinking and ignoring her. But didn't she see he was giving her everything she wanted, everything money could buy? And with her being fond of the gargle herself, who was she to talk about his drinking? And he was having a grand old time. After arriving with Theresa in Cork from Canada with no money, knowing nobody, he now owned a home in the country, co-owned commercial properties in the city, and had a successful insurance brokerage. They'd arrived back with nothing but his ambition. He'd beaten the odds! He was somebody-was the life of every party. Times were good!

Days and months floated into one another with time evaporating like morning dew until suddenly Brian was four.

By then Murphy's drinking knew no boundaries. Increasing numbers of clients began to phone, angrily asking why he'd yet again failed to show up for meetings. Fuck em. What if he lost a few accounts? Never mind, there'd be plenty more.

Increasingly he found himself making excuses when clients were in his office and the shakes began, then he'd frantically rush to the toilet to puke up the previous night's feed. But by late afternoon he'd feel his body reviving itself. Come five-thirty, he'd have convinced himself that a brandy or three would settle him. By seven he was fine again.

Then one afternoon, after being off on the piss for a few days, he stumbled into the Imperial Hotel on the South Mall and unfortunately bumped into Peader, his silent partner in business. He was a man who enjoyed a drink but never allowed it to get the better of him. Peader was from an impoverished Kerry family. He'd made his first fortune in America before returning to Ireland to make another. They had a good thing going. Apart from his silent partnership in the insurance brokerage and referring many clients, whenever he heard of a property for sale that was a good deal he'd call Murphy who'd buy it in his name, then they'd change the title a few months later thereby keeping his connection private. That was how they'd bought several commercial properties in Tuckey Street.

After his initial burst of enthusiasm, however, Peader had understandably begun to become fed up with Murphy's inconsistent work ethic and fondness for the gargle. He'd already expressed his displeasure at the fall in profits so it came as no surprise now when he pulled Murphy into a quiet corner and said, "This just won't do. People are talkin 'bout you and there's not much business being done. Can't go on ye know." Murphy had the good grace to feel embarrassed. Peader was correct, he'd become a liability and realized it. Murphy's parents had raised him better than to behave like such a boussey. "Have to dissolve the partnership an buy out yer interest in the properties." Peader's bushy eyebrows lifted skyward over eyes as cold as a winter morning. Self-pity mixed with self-loathing overwhelmed Murphy. He was embarrassed because he respected Peader and realized he'd messed up a wonderful opportunity.

He ordered another round of drinks and they sat in silence while around them boisterous laughter mocked his dark mood. He had another few drinks while Peader sipped on his. Suddenly the effects of the prior few month's excessive drinking sucked all the life force out of him. He was horrified to notice tears running down his cheeks. "What do you want to do, Peader?"

Unblinking eyes looked silently at Murphy, carefully taking his measure, then a piece of paper magically appeared in his ruddy hand and he wrote something while Murphy looked down at the floor. "Here sign this, it'll give ya money te go out completely on yer own, ease any financial pressure especially now with the baby, and you won't have te worry 'bout costly renovations te the properties an the like." Murphy didn't bother to read it-simply signed where Peader's finger pointed.

"An te make it legal I have to give ye a deposit, a consideration." With that he took out a wad of multicolored bills from his pocket, counted off five hundred pound in notes and shook Murphy's hand, marvelously beaming all the while. Moments later he was gone while Murphy remained staring into an empty glass that was quickly refilled.

When Murphy partially sobered up next day and read what he'd signed he got one hell of a shock. He would receive but a pittance for his share of the valuable properties. At first, he laughed at the humor of it all then became angry at being so blatantly duped. His fury against Peader was equaled with anger and disgust at himself. How could he have been so stupid? But surely the agreement couldn't possibly be legal? He spoke with a few solicitors on the South Mall and they weren't so sure. "But where's the justice, the equity in it?" he remonstrated. He soon found that their cautiousness cloaked another concern. Peader had become a powerful man in the community with serious social and political connections and Murphy, being a relative newcomer, a blow in, had none. No solicitor or barrister on the South Mall had the balls to take the case for fear of offending the 'Great Man.' He was referred to an excellent barrister in Middleton who could probably have helped but he refused to represent Murphy after his repeated failures to show up for appointments. Instead he got a newly qualified barrister with his arse barely wet.

When the case went to trial, it was held at the Cork City courthouse. The Irish love theater so the room was well packed with many faces Murphy recognized and even more he didn't. One person he did was Bill Walshe, a former drinking partner. He was representing Peader. It took a short time for the legal issue to be decided. The judge didn't bother to retire even momentarily to his chambers to consider the case. Peader's written agreement was ordained a validly binding legal document. "Both parties are ordered bound to the terms as outlined in the offer and acceptance," the judge pontificated in a lofty voice that reeked of a sock stuck in mouth. Drowning his sorrows Murphy went on a mighty tear. Three days later he rambled into the Imperial Hotel. In the bar, laughing horse like, was the honorable judge, while his companion Peader toasted his good health.

A month later, Murphy drove Theresa a few miles out the road from their home while the baby sat happily gurgling in her arms. What Theresa did not know was they were about to lose the house in foreclosure. Murphy was too cowardly to tell his wife about their fall in fortune. Making matters worse, he lied to her that they were going to sell the house and instead buy the lovely half acre of land facing the sea where they would live happily ever after.

They got out at the site and Brian hid in the tall grass and roared with laughter when Murphy chased him. He'd tickle Brian mercilessly if he caught him, and the boy's uncontrollable laughter made him collapse so then Murphy would kiss his belly and tickle his feet until he escaped and the pursuit began again.

Behind them Theresa kneeled as she rolled out a blanket, then removed sandwiches and a bottle of wine from the hamper.

Soon the three of them were happily munching, lost in their individual thoughts, and lulled by sounds of sea breaking against shoreline. Brian laughed and waved at the swallows which darted above, and threw crumbs to bright eyed, hovering seagulls. The generous summer sun nourished them as Theresa smiled contentedly over at her husband as she passed him another glass of wine.

He caught Brian's eye, and when he returned the smile, Murphy swore his son would always know how much he loved him. He'd break the Irish tradition of never holding him when he was beyond the toddler stage. His boy would never have to search furtively among gestures and silent innuendos to know the depth of his father's feeling for him. And he'd never be beaten. Brian would never experience humiliation and physical pain while bamboo sticks cut into him as he whimpered and sobbed knowing himself to be a bad and useless person. Brian would always know his father was there for him. Always.

"Better go, it's getting dark," said Theresa. Murphy saw them to the door at home. "I'll pick up a bottle. Be right back," he said. Theresa's beautiful eyes looked up at him and some words almost fell off her lips, but they didn't. Then he was gone and soon in the pub where alcohol flooded his veins with as fine a feeling as the afternoon's hot sun had been on his skin.

The final act of his downfall happened quickly.

One moment he was being invited into the inner circle and introduced as a bright man about town, now, especially after the court case, and his non-stop drinking, he was ostracized from all angles. It became normal for him to wake up with several days' worth of beard and find thick lumps of grass and mud clinging to the sides of his car while having no clue how it got there.

He rented a small office space and tried unsuccessfully to build his business. While he had been feted as a success, now everyone, apart from one friend, Trevor Whelan, deserted him. He still somehow managed to keep the house repossession from Theresa by getting to the post before she saw it. But time was fast approaching the eviction date. There was less than two thousand pounds in their account. He forged Theresa's signature on a check and, deciding it was time for him to disappear, he emptied the account.

His last view of Brian for many years was seeing him dressed in his pajamas crying at the window while Murphy drove out of his life, leaving his son and Theresa to fend for themselves.

Chapter Twenty-Five

PEPSI

Murphy woke with a jolt. A figure cautiously emerged from under the blankets. A woman, more of a girl really, stood in the semi darkness awkwardly clutching a pillow that partially covered her naked body. A fat moon passed by the window, momentarily lighting the room showing clothes scattered across the floor.

The girl smiled nervously while her lips absentmindedly chewed strands of long dark hair. Flickering images of the night drifted before Murphy as he tried to figure out who she was, how they had met.

The girl then squatted in a corner. "Jazus, tink I'm goin ta puke." she croaked in thick Limerick. He spotted a battered tin basket in the corner with a Woolworth's bag in it. "Puke in the bucket." Then he wanted her gone.

He still couldn't figure how they'd met he silently cursed his drinking that repeatedly led to these preposterous situations. Couldn't figure how and where he'd met her. Only a few days before he'd woken with a major hangover with dried blood on his face. Beside him lay a dormant walrus complete with moustache dangling on a quivering pair of lips inside which one black tooth hung sideways. The room trembled, the bed levitated each time she inhaled, rising effortlessly off the floor before descending loudly when she exhaled. She must have been fifty if she was a day and snored like a teapot on the boil, barely two horrifically close inches from Murphy's startled face. Terrified of waking the beast, he quietly plotted his escape but was immobilized by fear.

Finally succumbing to the gift of desperation, he slunk down by the side of the bed then. frantically grabbing whatever clothes, he could find, and one shoe, he ran out the bedroom door as if the devil was in pursuit. He had no idea how he'd gotten there. Now, a similar story This would have to stop.

Slowly he clawed through the thick cobwebs that cluttered his brain. Perhaps he'd met her yesterday in a pub while handing out sunflowers then gone with her on a tear? Her name was Ann or Patricia? She tried to puke but couldn't. "Put three fingers down your throat." She crawled on her hands and knees over to the window and pushed it open. The cold fresh air failed to cleanse the stench of cheap furniture and soiled, moth-eaten bedclothes. Empty takeaway boxes lay scattered over the faded linoleum floor. Murphy grabbed a whiskey bottle that still had some life in it. "Come here my darling." The girl looked back hopefully but he ignored her, instead reaching out and taking a deep slug, relishing the burning sensation as it reached raw deep inside then hit his brain.

There was no clock in the room but the buzz had worn off, so it was probably around four am. Repeatedly waking during the night was depressing. The loneliness only other alkies and druggies knew, the reminders of harming anyone who'd loved him, the futility of living, the great potential of his youth long wasted when he'd been a shining but now faded star. Soon he would hopefully wake up dead. The closest he came to prayer was asking God to let him die, preferably yesterday.

He searched impatiently for a towel and dried off the night's sweat, then greedily gulped more whiskey. It flowed deep and reached into his gut. It bit hard, a painful but reassuring medicine. Another slug and he was back on his way to temporary release.

"I'm Patricia, but you call me Pepsi." Then tentatively out came her hand for the whiskey bottle as she moved cautiously towards him. Murphy had wanted her gone but the recent blast from the whiskey made her look somewhat appealing. Perhaps he'd keep her a while, then be done with her.

He still hadn't figured how they'd met. "I lost the flowers ye gave me in de pub." That didn't help. She giggled again, beginning to sound easier on his ears and nicer to his bloodshot eyes. She had a sweet questioning smile. Another gulp and the whiskey finally kicked in making everything glow, the fear vanish. He wanted her again. The bed was soaked, so he moved to another. It smelled moldy, but at least was dry.

Then, in a rare moment of lucidity, he remembered meeting her. Yesterday afternoon it was. He'd been drinking all day meandering aimlessly trying unsuccessfully to get fucked up, the buzz stubbornly slow to settle in. His shoulder length hair and ankle length coat floated in the breeze, large yellow sunflower in lapel while he quoted Yeats, Patrick Kavanagh, and Oscar Wilde to anybody within ear's reach. He'd been handing out flowers to strangers, most who told him to get lost, when he found himself wandering down a narrow, cobbled alleyway and into a pub called the Gates of Hell, located behind the Franciscan church. It had been years since he'd done a streak from there. Drinking a Chivas, and with only two sunflowers left, he noticed her sitting on a stool at the bar, pint in hand, listening to some geezer while vigorously nodding her head. She was wearing a purple T-shirt, and a short skirt. He felt her welcoming eyes on him. They exchanged brief glances as he passed on his way to the jax.

Making his way back through the smoke covered crowd, he handed a sunflower to her and her man. She laughed "You're mad out." But her eyes and body language clearly welcomed his attention. If he wanted a ride, it was probably on. "Sebastian Dangerfield the third at your service,

Madam." As he exaggeratedly bowed. Her companion got nervous and, convinced Murphy was a headbanger, quickly finished his pint, then left. Murphy had taken the seat next to Patricia, or Pepsi, as he had apparently named her.

They had more scoops while exchanging irrelevant pleasantries and sniffing each other out, then toddled off on a pub-crawl in the older part of the town. He didn't want to go where people would recognize him. Only the day before, he'd been in bank to get money for drink, when he'd had an awkward moment with Padie Wheland, a one-time school friend. Padie had become a prosperous builder while Murphy was an unemployed drunk reeking of stale booze. "What are you up to?" asked Padie with a frown, wondering how outrageous the response would be. He wasn't disappointed. "Heading off soon to North Africa. Going to walk across the Sahara Desert." Perhaps Murphy believed it. Padie looked at him, silent, at a complete loss for words. "Have a good walk then." Off he went shaking his head, wondering about when the madness had settled on his childhood friend.

They headed over to the poorer part of town, down by the market place and old Limerick. But first they had to cross O'Connell Street. Passing by Roches Stores, he saw his father coming out of Cruises hotel dressed splendidly in an Old Crescent blazer with matching gray slacks. It must have been Monday because he was talking with other Rotary members. Murphy cowered behind a shop door and heard rather than saw his father's wonderful laugh, one he'd treasured since childhood. Quickly he pushed Pepsi inside Roches Department Store. They hid there, waiting until the group of men had walked far enough up O'Connell Street while locked deep in conversation.

He was tempted to say hello to his father. He hadn't been in contact for a long while. They didn't have a clue where he was. He was gutted about the pain that must be causing them. Perhaps he'd been killed on some far-off construction site. Regardless, he didn't want to embarrass his father in front of his Rotary friends. Truth be said, he also didn't want to have to face him and talk about life. What was the point? He was ashamed. Bottom line was, he'd fucked up. His birth was an aberration for his family. His death would be a welcome relief.

Pepsi and he drank their way through the remainder of the day. She amazed him with her capacity for the jar. Light began to fade so it must be getting late. They had made their unsteady way to a bar over in Irishtown and she was keeping pace with his drinking. Merciful hour, so young and drinking like that! The next bar was so small you could barely figure which glass was yours. The door, when it opened, provided glimpses of the River Shannon. Murphy counted three, no, four men wrapped in thick coats and wellies up beyond their waists, casting their lines out into midstream as they struggled against the swirling current and blinding rain. They were searching for the salmon that lurked, waiting to fight their way upstream and fulfil their destiny at the spawning grounds above Annacotty.

Across the river, Thomond Castle proudly stood. Murphy saw helmeted guards looking out the turrets, watching for the English armies to advance. He was nine years old again and it was parents' night at his Jesuit school. There were three lads on stage. Diarmuid Powell, Tim Killeen, and himself. They had been elected to speak about the replica of the Siege of Limerick his class had built. Murphy's turn to speak came and, although initially nervous, he loved it the moment he heard his voice reverberate through the hall. Later, in South's bar, he heard his father proudly say, "Before he got up to speak, I had my head in my hands, but by God, he did a grand job altogether." This as he ordered another round of drinks and threw Murphy an extra bag of Taytos, his eyes sparkling with pride. Impulsively he came over and ruffled his youngest son's hair. The child silently exploded with unstated joy. But now his eyes brimmed full with tears.

"How old do ya tink I am?" Pepsi brought him back to the present. "No idea." Not that he cared. "No, seriously, HOW OLD would ya say I am?" She gave him a cutting look that made him feel uncomfortable. Go away. "Doesn't matter. Don't care." Her cow sized eyes looked sadly at the ground. Jezz, he'd better humor her otherwise he'd never get a ride. "How old do you feel today?" She looked at him, puzzled. She paused for a moment, gulped down her pint, then sighed. "Today I feel old." "Then that's how old you are." "Turned seventeen last week," The nosey old timers at the bar swiveled their heads, noses twitching with interest. "Come on, let's go." He quickly led her away from the smirking stares.

Walked on past the Treaty Stone on which the Treaty of Limerick was signed, representing yet another broken English promise in Ireland's violent history. They rambled into the appropriately named Treaty bar. A game of forty-five was on. Murphy played for a while and always lost. T'was past closing time when they spilled out of the place and into the bitter night cold. "Where do you live?" He asked. "Sometimes at de Mount convent, sometimes oder places." She didn't want to say anything more and that was fine with Murphy. The less he knew about her the better. Neither had a place to sleep but by now, they were so fucked up from the drink it didn't matter. They rambled down by Clancy's Strand then turned left over Sarsfield's Bridge. Knackered, they paused to rest against a wall down by the docks. T'was there his Crescent schoolmate John, one sad night, had gone down the slippery steps and intentionally walked into the Shannon River. Murphy wondered about the horror of his torment must have been while taking that final, lonely walk to the dockside then down the cold, concrete steps. Perhaps he'd momentarily paused to reconsider, before deciding to kill himself rather than live in torment, preferring the cold, lonely waters of a turbulent river death over the irrationality of living.

"Know a place where we can git drink all night an also crash." Murphy welcomed the interruption. They walked over to the taxi ranks on Thomas Street and an annoyed taxi driver dropped them off only five blocks away at the Cecil Hotel. She knocked loudly on the door. Murphy wondered if she'd be able to get them in. She was plastered, unsteady on her feet, slurring her words. He was concerned she'd pass out before he had the chance to ride her.

A peephole opened. Whoever was behind it was smoking a cigarette from a tiny mouth that spewed sewer breath. "Oh, tis yerself Patricia, an a gintleman friend. Come in but keep quiet. Were raided only last week. Nice day for de races."

"He's Dinnis, de nite manager," Pepsi said in what she assumed was a low voice but could be heard in the next county. Dennis pulled back the gates of the kingdom and they gratefully entered. This man was a solid example of night life badly worn. His skeletal body was covered by a stained, black suit and a torn, red tie that lay thrown over his shoulder. He had eyes that winked at each other, reeked of booze, cigarettes, and impending disintegration. "D'owner is away at de Knights of Columbus national convention so I'm in charge." Dennis giggled, delighted with his elevated status. He ushered them into a dimly lit room that was smoky and welcomingly dark. Tony Bennett sang The Good Life" from a juke box. The irony was lost on all present. The room was sprinkled with an assortment of sadness, drunken couples desperately clinging to each other and individuals drinking the night through in solitary thought. Fortunately, Murphy recognized nobody.

After a few belts, the somber music took him over and he lost interest in Pepsi, instead floating abstractedly as contradictory images of sadness and happiness rapidly entered then emptied his addled brain. He put coins into the juke box and played Billy Holiday singing Strange Fruit three times in succession before being roared at to play it no more. He then melted into welcomed anonymity.

Pepsi recognized a friend of hers and went over to him. Murphy stayed busily drinking oblivious of her existence. "Tommy wants te take me home te his place." Grand. "What will you have to drink Tommy before you two leave?" He'd no more interest in this creature. After buying them a drink, he left the bar and arranged a room to crash in.

Before leaving, Tommy went to the jax while Pepsi staggered across the room to Murphy. "Sebastian, I want te be wit you." "Well you're with yer man." "Tellin him I'm goin wit you'.' The corners of her mouth drooped as she said this and spittle dripped down her chin. Tears began forming in her eyes. Jesus, she was about to start bawling. Tommy came out of the jax zipping up his trousers. "Cop on, will you?" Murphy urged. She glared unsteadily at him, took a deep breath then turned dramatically to Tommy her long hair dancing around her head. "Changed my mind. Stayin wit Sebastian." She was pure brazen. That was the last thing Murphy wanted especially as Tommy was understandably disturbed by the sudden disappearance of his ride, one Murphy had absolutely no interest in. And there was no glory to be had in fighting; it hurt no matter who did the beating. "I'm out of here. She's all yours Tommy." He tried unsuccessfully to detach her arms and give her to Tommy who was glaring daggers and seemed ready to rumble. She remained a knot around his neck. Inexplicably Tommy began to laugh. "Ah te hell wit her, she's useless now anyway." Then away with him leaving Pepsi smiling brightly while still clinging to an unamused Murphy.

Dennis who, as night manager, had over the years observed all human and often inhuman behavior, silently observed the game unfold while smiling quietly through a smoky cloud. By now Murphy had moved to a high level of intoxication his brain cells exploding and creating a mixture of delight and depression throughout every cell of his body. Stuck with the girl, he bought a bottle of Powers whiskey, then helped her up the carpet-less stairs toward room 311 which for some reason was on the fifth floor. She was beginning to pass out. He was about to leave her unconscious on the floor then decency kicked in. "Stay awake, come on I've got a bottle with me." She began to ramble incoherently, and would hopefully soon be asleep. She began to pass out just as they arrived at the bedroom door. He dragged her inside, lay her down on the bed. She was muttering something he couldn't make out. "Na, dat's fine." He enjoyed drunk women but not hopelessly drunk ones. They cried uncontrollably while obsessing over the sadness of their useless lives, their heads messed up and their bodies dead weight. He usually kept a distance from such hags. Fortunately, she immediately passed out.

He turned on a battered radio that sat on a broken chair. The Animals wailed, "We've got to get out of this place if it's the last thing we ever do, girl, there's a better life for me and you." Murphy opened the whiskey bottle and sighed in relief as the alcohol continued its subtle but deadly journey. The Augustinian Church nearby chimed four bells. So it was four-o clock. Not bright for another few hours. Then the town's inhabitants would rise from slumber and begin their sensible day, one that would change little for the rest of their pathetic lives until they finally croaked and went to their promised, eternal reward. To Murphy it condemnation to a life sentence of boring repetition, each day repeating itself, same woman, same job, same small town with a penny looking down on a half penny, small predictable everything, until the final release when no next day happened.

Murphy heard himself laughing at the irony of his condemnation. He'd been drinking day and night for months now but had no idea how to stop even if he wanted to. How much longer could he go on getting high, then low, then high, desperately clinging to the buzz until passing out. What would he do when the money was gone or the high no longer happened? Then where would he hide?

But in this moment, a distraction was available. Pepsi lay snoring on one of the beds. Her body had become more appealing as the golden whiskey soothed him. He watched the streetlight touch her face through the window. She half smiled, then her forehead and eyebrows wrinkled as she dreamed. A pretty one all right with long black hair tumbling over a pretty face and rich lips made for enjoyment. She seventeen, he thirty-two, both ancient. He filled a bucket full with cold tap water and emptied it over her. Startled, she shivered, looked around, looking scared, not knowing where she was. Slowly, she recognized Murphy standing in the half-light by the window.

"Sorry I passed out before ya had me." She greedily eyed the bottle before reaching for it and lifting it quickly to her mouth. She slugged it down. Pushing her onto the bed she lay spread wide clutching the bed sheets as he poured whiskey over her, watching it flow like a river to the ocean. He wanted to lose himself inside her and disappear forever. He found himself alternating between primal ecstasy and strange tenderness for this girl who moaned under him. Then she started crying, sobbing loudly, and babbling incoherently. Angrily he moved away from her and drank deeper while ignoring her pleas for comfort.

More church bells roared breaking the morning stillness. Six o'clock, time for first mass. Dawn now. First light streaked its way across the eastern sky, intruding, uninvited, as they lay silently under the foul-smelling bedsheets.

That was the first of many sorrowful nights Murphy and Pepsi would experience together in that shoddy building.

All too soon came a banging sound on their bedroom door. "Time te check out. One hour past checkin' out." Loud, angry intrusive sounds repeated every five minutes each time with greater urgency. "Out in a minute." "Come on, we'd better get up." There was a shower down the hall and he headed for it. The water fluctuated between various degrees of hot and cold as it cleansed his body making him feel somewhat alive.

Walking up Cecil Street, Pepsi suggested they drop in for a farewell drink in Flannery's bar. Murphy liked the bar. it had nooks and crannies that provided refuge from prying eyes. The owner had a variety of classical music records which she always played even while competing with sports on the telly. The orchestra of St. Martin in the Fields playing Vivaldi's Four Seasons conducted by Neville Mariner provided an interesting contrast to the punters excited voices. Being knowledgeable about horses, Murphy placed a few bets. Pepsi, who didn't know how many legs a horse had, picked three winners, while his still hadn't finished the next day.

Later, but not too soon, it was dark outside. He left Flannery's pub with a bottle of Powers whiskey tucked carefully under one arm, and Pepsi hanging off the other. They made their way back down the street and booked in for another night in the Cecil Hotel. Avoiding the bar, they headed straight to bed. He felt a sense of relief at again having a place to sleep. Although Pepsi was no virgin, she'd begun at thirteen with a priest visiting the orphanage, she was clumsy and surprisingly lacking in sexual knowledge. Murphy delighted in how enthusiastically she learned how to please him and herself.

Next morning, after his usual breakfast of Bulmer's cider, then a gin & tonic, inspiration hit him. "I'll go and live in Greece. Dip my toes in the Aegean Sea. Drink wine with the Gods. Greece is a grand place altogether and relatively inexpensive." He blabbered to a confused and disinterested barman. Sadly, he couldn't have summoned up the energy to cross the road, let alone travel across Europe. Dropping quickly from elation to depression, realizing the insanity of his proposal, he instead gave all his money to Dennis, asking him to keep track of it and deduct his expenses until it was all gone. "I'll mind it fer ye Sebastian. No worries." Smiled Dennis, delighted with his unexpected bounty.

Time became immeasurable. Daylight came sometimes with surprising speed then at other times with turtle like slowness. He didn't know how long they stayed at the Cecil, perhaps two, three months, perhaps one. The only daylight they ever saw was through the hotel bar windows or their manky bedroom upstairs. The highs were becoming hard to get and harder to maintain. He lay terrified as the fucked-up feeling left him then demanded to be refueled only to turn on him and become less accessible. He kept waking after increasingly shorter sleeps then staring mindlessly at the paint chipped ceiling. He began to know the time of the night by the sounds that emanated from the streets and alleyways. His skin began to crawl twisting him inside and out. He regularly screamed, begging for death. It was living not dying that terrified him. He needed to be dead before the money was gone. He thought of stealing a car and crashing but figured he's fail and instead survive as a paraplegic doomed to be fed from a straw for the next fifty years.

He used Pepsi occasionally but had lost interest in extensive activity with her while she now constantly wanted him. She was afraid because of his loss of interest he'd dump her. Then she'd have to find someone else to support her habit. She would do anything, everything, to retain his interest. She begged to pleasure him in any way he might want. Her offers were met with cold rejection.

The inevitable morning came when Dennis told him he only had enough funds for one more night. Armed with that news, he proceeded to go on one final almighty pissup. Next day they left the Cecil with only enough for a few drinks for him, none for her. He vaguely wondered where he'd sleep that night. Not that he cared. His only concern was where he'd get money for the next drink. Now he was broke, he told Pepsi to provide funds, otherwise fuck off.

She came back five hours later and handed over several crumpled notes. He rewarded her with a double brandy. Then they went back on the piss.

Chapter Twenty-Six

SQUATTING

There were four of them when he was sober, unknown numbers when wasted. Night time was scariest when he could only hear, not see, them as they scurried along the sides of the walls. Then they'd stop for varying times while exchanging chat, perhaps deciding on a strategy how best to eat him. He'd become the menu for a rat's banquet. Terrified, unable to move, he struggled not to fall asleep.

He'd been wandering homeless around Cork town for several weeks or perhaps months living in abandoned buildings, eating from thrown out food behind restaurants, begging on street corners for spare change and drinking the cheapest wine. One morning a former business colleague dropped coins into Murphy's tin can. Murphy no longer bore the slightest resemblance to the smartly dressed, successful business man he'd once been. He'd lost two stone in weight, itched constantly from sores on his body, his stomach pained from what might be ulcers, his teeth constantly darted pain from broken fillings and beatings he'd got while drunk.

His luck seemed to change when a former drinking friend told him about a vacant place to crash. It was in Douglas about three miles from where he had slept the night before. He tried to get on a bus but was refused because he smelt so badly and his clothes were manky. Somehow, he managed to walk to Douglas over a few hours, got there before darkness and felt well rewarded for his efforts.

The house was a well-ordained detached bungalow with well laid out gardens similar to those where he'd lived before his fall from grace. He stood silently in the gathering gloom watching, wondering. There was no sign of life inside. It looked safe. He walked up the path then around to the back where he broke a small window to gain access. What were the stories of the people who had lived there? It didn't matter a hoot provided they didn't come back while he was there.

Inside, the house seemed lifeless, no furniture and with an overpowering smell of disuse. Everything had been removed except for one small dry jam jar with the corpses of flowers drooping from its mouth. Exhausted he laid his body on the bare wood floor, wrapped his overcoat tightly for warmth before gratefully passing out.

Later, under cover of darkness, he rambled over to the same chipper he'd visited for years after the pubs closed. And what a great chipper it was! Run by some religious sect, they were always polite and disgustingly happy, smiling even when drunks roared impatiently for service. They had the best fish and chips in Cork. Once upon a time, when he had money and people to drink with, Turkey O'Brien offered his philosophy after the pubs had closed. "Ye know lads, one of life's great joys is comin out of the pub havin lashings of porter, headin to the chipper, putting on the old feed bag, then diggin into fresh cooked cod, mushy green peas, a bag of chips all of it steaming hot, mixed with an abundance of tomato sauce, a suggestion of salt and vinegar; the whole of it wrapped in yesterday's newspaper. Then, if yer lucky," he'd continued between mouthfuls of fish and licking his greasy fingers, "you find an understandin girl an finish the night off with a decent ride." But that was a lifetime ago. Now all he hoped for or cared about was a place to sleep for the night. He checked to see if anyone was watching before quickly walking to the back of the house. Never having squatted before, he was concerned about being caught under embarrassing circumstances that would confirm his departure from society.

With no electricity, he sank onto the floor cursing his negligence in forgetting candles to lighten the darkness. Soon he sensed the presence of other life. Probably mice but, to his horror, when he lit a match he saw several rats smiling complacently at him. The remaining three matches quickly died. He shivered with fear and cold while wrapping his overcoat tighter.

The fish and chips were getting cold. Hunger overcame his fear so he quickly devoured everything except the bones which he wrapped inside the oily newspaper then threw in the direction of where the rats sounded to be. He took a long gulp from the remaining wine bottle and staggered hastily from the room. The scarpering sounds of the rats followed him down the hall.

Keeping down and away from all streetlights Murphy peeked through the letterbox and saw the last of the people leaving the pubs and lines outside the chipper. Lots of chat, laughing and craic outside there now. It'd be loud for a while as the lads let off some steam and old wounds become reopened under the confusing influence of Bacchus. Soon children would be cuddled, some women loved gently while others would be forced to endure the clawing embraces of foul smelling, dribbling, bollixes of husbands who'd demand their women conform to their sacramental vows and provide the men their legal rights. When those poor wives went to the priest for protection they would be told to shut up and obey their marriage vows. They would get their reward in the next life, if not in this.

Murphy sat huddled in his coat realizing he was the outsider. He didn't belong in society that night nor would he ever in the future. The lights in the chipper went out. Now there was no sound in the world except the occasional dog barking, or a car with a satisfied or frustrated romancer returning home from the chase. It would remain silent until round six o'clock in the morning when the Church bells all over Cork from Shandon down to the Lough would ring out proclaiming a new day. But now all was quiet. The night was left to Murphy and the rats who salivated while waiting for him to fall asleep.

Chapter Twenty-Seven

THE LONGFELLAH DIES

"She's already been fitted for her widow's clothes," his sister whispered at the hospital door. As they approached his father's room three women were leaving. Varying from about thirty to forty, all very attractive, all crying their hearts out. "Who were those women?" wondered his mother as they watched the ladies collective wiggle their way down the hospital corridor. They looked back furtively, before quickly disappearing around a corner. "Oh, dad knows a lot of people. They're probably on some committee with him, or know him through Rotary, or the golf or rugby club." He didn't know if she believed him. Somewhat coldly she responded, "I see, said the blind man."

The room his dying father had was the last stop for hopeless cases, also known as God's waiting room. If you were put there, you came out feet up into a hearse. Murphy wondered if they were too late. His father lay still, with his denture-less mouth wide open. Murphy found humor at the idea of the toothless lover being the ladies last sight of their Casanova.

His mother sat by the bed looking at her quickly fading husband of fifty years. She held his hand in the first display of affection Murphy had ever seen between them. "Now, Michael, you're going on a journey. You can see a shining white light. Don't be afraid. Walk toward it." She gazed intently at her husband's face guiding him towards his departure from this life.

His father had been found a few days before,

collapsed, arms by his sides, lying unconscious in the grass across from the cottage where Jamsie O'Malley and his mother had once lived. The years of challenging his body's capacity to absorb unbelievable volumes of alcohol had finally caught up. He'd been carted away in an ambulance to the Regional hospital.

His three children stood around the bed, silent, lost in their private thoughts. Father Frank, an old family friend, was also present. He administered the last rites. Murphy doubted he'd heard a full confession as he had only been there an hour before his father slipped into a deep coma. Part of his view of the nonsensical nature of religion was how forgiveness for sins worked. If dying, and unable to make a formal confession, you can simply whisper you are sorry for your sins then the entire debit sheet would be wiped clean, automatically canceling out hell and purgatory, and swinging the gates of heaven wide open for you. But if one did not live to utter those precious words and had the same list of sins as the other person, then it's to hell for eternity.

He found it hard to believe his once indestructible father was dying. The body on the bed didn't even seem like the larger than life man he'd loved and admired. A rattling sound came from his father's throat as he struggled in his final moments. Murphy watched tears stream down his mother's face. She clasped her husband's hand tighter and softly whispered, "Michael, oh Michael, dear Michael." Father Frank raised his hand, muttered words in Latin, then made the sign of the cross. Murphy stole a quick look at his siblings. Grainne had her hands crossed, praying, stoic and unbreakable as ever. Liam stood upright hands clasped, head bowed down and quietly crying. Murphy wanted to, but could not, reach out and comfort him.

His father's eyelids fluttered weakly, then very slowly opened. "Where in the name of Jeeeeesus am I?" He asked, looking around with immense interest. "Oh, sorry

Father Frank."

His mother quickly withdrew her hand. The tears stopped flowing. A look of consternation and horror spread over her now rigidly upright body. You'd swear somebody had shoved a red-hot poker up her arse. In the blink of an eyelid, her dreams of being fitted for her black widow's outfit had been rudely snatched from her. Gone were the sympathetic handshakes from neighbors while she held eyes downcast humbly accepting God's will. Access finally, to money without having to ask for it, and feeling humiliated when questioned about the amount of grocery bills. Perhaps worst of all, she, as the dutiful wife, would have to nurse the blackguard back to health. Withdrawing her hand, she remained silent and grew pale while contemplating life's cruelty.

His father miraculously recovered with no apparent brain damage. His team of doctors were astonished, all shaking their heads at the improbability of it all. Within weeks, he was in the pub regaling audiences about his close brush with death. An obituary had appeared in the Limerick Leader and he demanded and received a retraction. The editor apologized to him, then off went the two of them on a tear. It was a grand story and they had a fine ole time in the pubs on the strength of it. His father loved carrying that retraction around with him and would happily produce it at the drop of a hat.

Mortality, as always, had the last laugh. Pancreatic cancer was confirmed in January. By April, he was in the ground.

In accordance with tradition, he went to his daughter's home to die. The night he passed, it was Murphy's turn to watch over him. He was in a deep coma. Liam told him their father had been calm for hours, barely breathing. The room was shrouded in the patient silence that waits on death's imminent arrival. It was dark apart from candles flickering little tongues of irregular light. Murphy looked at the shrunken body and, while holding his father's hand, thought about the special times they'd shared. He felt deep regret over the pain and heartache he'd caused his parents.

There was slight movement in the bed. His father opened his eyes, looked groggily at Murphy, then softly, "God bless you." Unspoken words of love, understanding, and forgiveness for his startled son. He briefly held Murphy's startled gaze before his grip softened and his life ended.

Chapter Twenty-Eight

FUNERAL

His mother didn't attend the funeral. Murphy barely made it himself. The week before he'd collected his mother from Croom where she'd been recovering after a hip replacement. The plan was for her to visit her dying husband to say goodbye before heading on to a convalescent home. But when they arrived at his sister's house and he opened the car door, his mother refused to move. "I can't go in, Lovey," she abruptly told him with tears streaming down from eyes wild with panic and sadness.

Murphy was in a quandary. Before collecting his mother, he'd called Grainne who had confirmed their father was all spruced up and anxious to see his wife. His sister would be furious if he failed to bring her in with father less than thirty yards away, sitting propped up and waiting. Although nobody had told him he was terminally ill, he probably knew only a short time was left to him. Murphy wondered what they would say to each other. Would they express regret at the wasted and painful years? Knowing they would never see each other again, would they break down, ask forgiveness, hold each other, express words of regret, affection, perhaps even of love? He laying wasted from cancer, she barely able to move, and even then, in great physical pain. Two old people, their life cycle almost completed, fifty years of a marriage that had died long before them.

Sitting distraught in the car, his mother tightly squeezed his hands. "Please, Lovey, please." she looked beseechingly up at him. He'd become the parent, she the child. Impulsively he held her awkwardly in his arms and gently rocked her as she wept. "It's all right, Mum, you don't have to do it." He smoothed the blanket over his mother's legs and closed the door on her and her visit. As they were driving away his father appeared at the window being held by his sister. He smiled as he waved goodbye.

When their father died a week later, both brothers drove out to the convalescent home to break the news. Her room faced onto the parking lot and when she saw them, her hand flew up to her mouth. As they entered she nodded her head then whispered, "He's gone, isn't he?"

The night before the funeral Murphy took a rake of his mother's valium. Despite recurring images of his father interrupting his sleep, the pills worked well, too well and, with the mass at ten, he suddenly woke from a stormy sleep. It was a quarter to ten. Without bothering to wash, he quickly dressed, then groggily drove at high speed to the church. Half an hour late he stumbled through the church doors. The ceremony was almost over. Heads turned. Grainne gave him the same withering look she'd given him years earlier when he'd stumbled in the door of the same church late for another service. Back then he was supposed to be Godfather at the baptism of her oldest daughter. On the innocent baby's behalf, he was scheduled to renounce the Devil and all his evil works, but he'd arrived too late and very drunk.

This time he was supposed to have read from the scripture, but he'd failed to honor even that basic task. The walk up the side of the church took a lifetime as hundreds of disapproving faces glared in disgust at the revolting failure of a son. Finally, he joined his siblings and relatives in the front pew. Six priests were assisting the Bishop of Limerick to say the mass. His father lay in an open oak coffin, hands crossed and looking very well considering the day that was in it. He was wearing a Rotary pin on the lapel of an elegant dark suit and with it a matching Old Crescent club rugby tie. Murphy kept waiting for him to sit up and ask for a pint.

At communion time Murphy was one of the few who didn't walk up to the altar rails with bowed head and folded hands. That brought yet more disapproving stares. Believing it to be, at best, a piece of stale bread, he almost bowed came to the unstated pressure, but the stubborn part of him refused to participate in the nonsense.

A police car escorted the convoy of cars out to the cemetery. The bishop rambled on about ashes to ashes, his father now being in a better place and sitting at the right hand of God. Murphy thought that, in the unlikely possibility an afterlife existed, his father would more likely be in heaven's pub having a whiskey while pretending not to check out female angels. With prayers finished, the gleaming casket was carefully lowered into the gaping hole. Solemn faces, many with tears, surrounded the graveside. Silence was broken only by occasional sobbing, while birds danced and twittered above. Pieces of clay thudded off the casket. Murphy took a flower from a wreath, threw it and watched as a sudden breeze caught it, making it dance momentarily before floating down into the pit. Goodbye father. He wanted to cry, but knowing he was being watched he refused to cheapen his father's memory by wallowing in any public display of grief. There would be plenty of time later when alone.

A large number of guests were invited back to his brother's home for food and refreshments. The Bishop, most of the priests celebrating the mass, and a few captains of industry stayed for a while. Shortly after they'd gone the craic began. Friends of his father from his acting days at the College Players theater group were there as were some of his musician friends. Murphy remembered his father telling him about the days when he, Mother and a bunch of the theatrical group used to cycle sixty miles to Kilkee. Although they were then in their late twenties, few of them owned cars and, besides, the war was on so petrol was scarce. At nighttime in Kilkee they'd go out beyond the Pollock Holes to the Amphitheater. It was, and still is, circular in shape and juts out over a hundred and fifty feet above an Atlantic Ocean that constantly pounds the coastline. It was there they used to light enormous fires that lit up the night sky for miles around. Every person was then required to either sing from a Gilbert and Sullivan musical or a piece from an opera, tell a story, play music, or recreate a part from some play they'd previously performed. Murphy smiled while thinking about the unique beauty and effortless creativity of those innocent times.

Now his brother's house and gardens were filled with music, singing and dancing as the drink flowed and met its mark. With increasing intensity fiddles, tin whistles, banjoes, a bowran and Uillean pipes floated notes high into the night air. Days later Murphy discovered that later some of the musicians had returned to the graveside, stood together in a circle, and played soft tunes and laments. They continued playing until dawn broke. Murphy would have happily exchanged years of his own life for the opportunity to have observed that celebration.

Since his father was the eldest of eleven children, Murphy was part of a large extended family. This had resulted in a childhood overflowing with seemingly never ending family interactions. There were constant baptisms, communions, and confirmations to attend. Earlier on there was the occasional funeral, then with the passage of time, more frequent burials. In childhood, he'd been terrified yet fascinated by the countrywomen dressed in black shawls who wailed dramatically as they sat lamenting the deceased's departure and helping guide the spirit into the afterlife.

Today the people attending his father's wake included many of his relatives. Looking at them was like walking backwards into his youth. His brothers, Murphy's uncles, were a lively bunch to say the least: his lone sister Pearl on whose farm Murphy had spent memorable summers, cousins he hadn't seen for years, all grown now and with families of their own running around causing joyous bedlam.

Eventually the gathering broke up. Murphy remained for as long as possible hoping his brother or sister would invite him to stay longer, or, even better, to offer an invitation to stay overnight. They had their families and each other for comfort; he had nobody, was an outsider, and alone. No invitation was forthcoming.

His "I'll be off so." Was met with no resistance.

He went back to his mother's house and sat with memories as companions. With his mother away for another week and his father dead, the house was eerily silent. He sat in his father's favorite lounging seat. Many a time Grainne and he had argued for the right to comb father's hair as he half snoozed after lunch. There usually was a shilling reward for doing it. Other memories floated before him but tears stung and he wanted no more of them. Instead he drove to Fennessy's pub and, sitting alone, he silently raised a glass to his father's memory.

Seeking a reason to delay returning to a silent house, he headed home the long way and, driving down by Punch's Cross, who did he spot but Pepsi striding along in all her glory. He hadn't been with her for a long time but since he had no one, now he sought her company.

"We buried my father today."

"He's dead?"

"Hopefully. Will you come with me?"

"Where?"

"Anywhere. I'm buying."

Her eyes lit up and she leaped into his car. He drove to the Davin Arms. Pepsi was gasping for a drink and quickly downed a few pints followed by a large gin and tonic before she began to relax. He had another Lucozade. Now that he was sober, their usually relaxed line of communication had been severed. She rambled on about her calamitous life, which sounded even sadder than it had been during their time together.

Murphy bought a bottle of vodka before returning to his place in Adare where he lit a decent fire that warmed them well. He badly wanted to talk about his father and his love for him, but no words came. Instead he remained silent. He felt completely nonsexual and awkward. Instinctively Pepsi seemed to understand. "Come on, let's go," she suggested, then took him to bed, held him in her arms as she stroked his hair while placing butterfly kisses on his forehead. For perhaps an hour, in between deep gulps from the vodka bottle, she rocked his trembling body while also drying his tears. Then she passed out while he remained awake until close to dawn.

When he woke, Pepsi was gone along with all the cash in his wallet. He smiled and wondered which pub she was in.

Chapter Twenty-Nine

LIMERICK 1985

People in that village masquerading as a city, where everybody knew what you'd done before you'd thought of doing it, now looked at Murphy with contempt. Childhood friends and former business associates crossed the street to avoid him. He understood, couldn't fault them for it. He might have reacted the same had their positions been reversed. He began to mirror their behavior, avoiding all contact, and became expert at scanning a street for confirmation it was safe to walk. He found himself turning into shops pretending to look at magazines, or standing motionless as a scarecrow looking with intense concentration into a store window, examining merchandise he had no intention or ability to buy. By doing this he could avoid direct contact with a world where he no longer belonged. In a short time span he had successfully navigated his way from consummate insider to social outcast.

He'd stopped drinking by going cold turkey then applied for many jobs, any job. But with unemployment in Ireland exceeding twenty per cent, his options were limited. Having no college education, or a trade, didn't help. Options were not improved by his reputation as a hopeless drunk. He did get one interview as a trainee manager for Kentucky Fried Chicken in O'Connell Street and dressed in a suit, shined shoes and a cheerful smile that didn't last long. He was horrified to be interviewed by pimply-faced children whose mothers should have immediately put them into prams and brought them home. They were clearly disinterested before telling him, in less than five minutes, they'd be in contact which clearly they never would. Having once owned a restaurant he felt humiliated. Walking past the monument to Daniel O'Connell he realized extreme action was required. The solution that came was simple if unnerving. He found a phone booth and asked his mother to meet him next day at the Galleon Grill.

He hadn't spoken to her since he'd left her home over a month before. Now he sat nervously watching her come towards him. She carried a Roche's store bag in one hand, and the perennial umbrella held tightly under the other armpit. She never traveled without it. Once they'd gone on a family holiday to a place in Spain that hadn't seen rain in summertime for over a hundred years. Despite that, she still insisted on taking her umbrella. You never know when I might need it," she'd said with absolute conviction. They had spent the first three days in Spain, sheltering from the storms and lashing rain with a deliriously gloating mother. On this dry, balmy, Irish spring day, she had her head protected by a heavy red scarf and blue overcoat that went well below her knees down to legs that were warmed by thick brown tights covered in turn by a sturdy pair of leather boots.

Not surprisingly, since his father's death, she'd begun to look better. Despite her problems in life, or perhaps because of them, she insisted on being turned out well whenever she left the house. "You never know when you might end up in hospital." She'd cheerfully comment. And on the several occasions she'd gone to Barrington's hospital, she would first have a manicure; pedicure and have her hair permed. Then she'd arrive at the reception desk looking glamorous as if heading to a function. Inside her suitcase would be a carton of Rothmans cigarettes that she would smoke during her brief hospital visit. Since she always had a private room, and was otherwise a model patient, the nurses tolerated it.

Both mother and son were uncomfortable. When she put her bags down Murphy heard bottles rattle from one of them. His mother sat across the table, one hand repeatedly moving back and forth from her open mouth as she puffed furiously on a flaming hot cigarette. An inch of ash accumulated in silence before spilling onto the blue checkered tablecloth.

She continued to study the menu, but he already knew what she would order. Finally, she smiled up at the patient waitress and asked for, "A tomato sandwich with onion, lettice, and a pot of Barry's tea, please."

They talked about safe generalities. "Seen Grainne and Liam lately?" "How's Peggy Barrett these days?" "Any scandal on the Avenue?"

Her meal arrived. Soon teeth, strong, but yellowed by years of smoking, were delicately nibbling on her tomato sandwich.

Half way through, she looked at him. "You have something to tell me?"

Pause, then out with it. "I'm off to America."

She froze then slowly put her sandwich down. He observed her gathering her resources, then came the inevitable tirade. "You do realize, don't you, there's a terrible shortage of jobs over there! I've heard people are starving, especially the newcomers." He knew she was picturing him, within days of arriving in that distant country, dressed in tattered clothes, being forced to stand in a soup line begging for slops and moldy bread. She shook her head, first from side to side, then up and down with gathering conviction. "There's nothing over there for you."

"What's for me here? We've got over twenty per cent unemployment."

"But its home. It's Ireland."

"Here's a reality check for you. They don't want to know me at the club. I've no degree, trade, or skill. There's people with college degrees digging ditches, and that's only if they have pull to get the job. Who'd employ me, and what would I work at? And did you hear I'm still said to drink a bottle of whiskey every morning before breakfast? To put it bluntly, I'm unemployable. I'm done here. You often said Irish children were simply cattle raised for export. Well, now it's time for the boat, or in my case, the plane."

"You don't have papers to work in America, do you?"

With a wave of his hand, he casually dismissed that minor inconvenience. "I've a multiple entry visa that allows me to visit as a tourist for up to six months. Will get a job no problem."

"How will you survive? Where will you live? Do you mind me asking how much money you have?"

"Enough to get by till I start a job." He would have ninety punts to his name when arriving into America.

She gave him the longest, lingering look. Resignation finally settled on her. She sat back, wondering why life had gone so wrong for her once golden boy. He took her silence as acceptance. He was emigrating, about to start a new life in a place he'd never been, an ocean and a continent away from her and his own son. He felt a heavy weight of sadness settle on him. Despite his destructive behavior, she felt closest to her youngest child. She would be lonely without his questionable presence in her life. Hesitantly, she asked him to come home for his remaining days in Ireland. He reluctantly agreed. It was the least he could do for her. Once there had been five people living there, many noisy parties and great craic. She told him she was thinking of selling and moving to an apartment.

For his final meal, she cooked steak and served it on formal dinnerware reserved for special occasions. The meat was accompanied by fluffy spuds and peas covered in butter and thick, steaming Bisto gravy. While the meal tasted delicious it was accompanied by a serving of unspoken emotions, each wanting to, but unable to express love, regret, or say anything of a substantive nature. He promised he'd call her after he'd landed safely in California. "And I'll always keep in touch." While thinking he might not. She said nothing, simply looked across the table with a look of unspoken sadness. His heart went out to her. He wanted to express his love, his regret at all the harm he'd done, but nothing other than banalities fumbled from his mouth. Neither was capable of overcoming their culturally reserved inhibitions. He bled for any Irish mother with a child who emigrated. It was an evil form of slow torture wondering about their child, never knowing where he was, how he was, or, after months of silence, wondering if he was alive.

Before going to bed, he went into his father's room. Opening the closet, he found his fencing saber and mask. They used to play fencing in the garden when he was a child, with Murphy using a big stick to fight. His father could beat him every time but occasionally let him win. Impulsively he put on the face mask and was again a child playing with his father, laughing, and shouting at each other. First the kiss to their deadly weapons, then the loud, "On guard!" Lunging, feinting, dodging before his father's foil would inevitably strike Murphy's heart and he'd would roar in denial. "No, Daddy it didn't hit me, honestly." They'd repeat the process a few more times until even the child couldn't deny the legitimacy of his towering father's strikes. They'd then disengage and formally bow to each other.

He entered the bedroom he'd slept in for the first eighteen years of his life and for years on and off since then. This was where he'd come, at age thirty-two, to rest up and detox. If his parents had not allowed him back home that time, he's have been homeless again and would probably have died on the streets.

Even though he'd disgraced them, his parents never chastised him. He wondered how many would have accepted their son back. And yet, when he'd gone away to college at thirty and in over two years had turned his life around, no drinking, admired and successful, they'd chosen to ignore his accomplishments, claiming he was simply playing at being a student. No, they'd never condemned him for his disgraceful behavior, but were also incapable of viewing him in any positive light. Maybe in a perverse way, his transgressions had been one thing connecting them to each other, something they always shared whatever else came between them? Had he perhaps been of some redemptive value to them if only for that?

Lying in his childhood bed, he tried to block out the past, the future. The former ashamed him, the latter terrified him. He'd destroyed everybody who'd loved him, had been born with talent and opportunity and had squandered everything. He knew nobody in America, would be there illegally, had enough money for a week at best. If deported, had nothing to return to.

Birds over in the nun's place chirped happily in the trees as they had done for generations past. The horn from the factory blew at ten o'clock just as it had done since his childhood. Alone in his bed, he lay motionless. This would be his final night ever sleeping at home. His mind reluctantly considered the adventure he was about to undertake. He'd have to bluff his way past the immigration people, had no papers to work, knew nobody in San Francisco, had no place to stay, had almost no money. Butterflies rumbled uncomfortably in his stomach as he tossed and turned throughout a restless night. He was frightened, no he was terrified, repeatedly waking after only a few minutes' restless sleep bathed in sweat, looking blankly into the darkness immobilized by fear of the future.

Hearing his mother moving about restlessly in her room interrupted his thoughts. If she fell from her bed on this night, he'd rush in, pick her up, cradle her in his arms, rock her gently, perhaps cry a little with her, kiss away her tears before placing her safely in bed. Then he would sit beside her until sure she was safely resting for the remainder of the night.

Chapter Thirty

EXILE'S RETURN

Thompson's Funeral Parlor, Limerick, Ireland

He kissed his mother Moya for the first and last time. Her dry, wrinkled forehead tasted colder than a bitter December morning. His expressionless eyes never left her carcass as his chilled lips moved up from her motionless face. He stepped back from the brown oak coffin in which she, having no other option, lay motionless. Beside him stood his brother and sister, two statues offering automated responses to those paying their final respects.

He imagined his mother carefully checking to see who had turned up and, more importantly, who had not. She alternated between pleased smiles and sad reflection at present and absent friends and neighbors.

With hand on mouth, she gasped at the bill for her funeral casket while vigorously shaking her grey head, horrified by the disgraceful waste of money. But he knew full well she would have been more distraught if the coffin had not been of a quality worthy of her perceived status in life.

She was dressed in a light brown, checkered dress. It was what she'd been wearing the last time he'd seen her alive. He wondered if she'd approve of the choice what with her being defenseless on display for all the world to gawk at. Her hair had been carefully styled and her nails varnished to tastefully match the dress. Always conscious of appearance, she would have been mortified had it been otherwise. As if praying, she held her old rosary beads in hands that rested over her still slim waist.

A procession of people quietly moved past her coffin. He hadn't seen any of them since he'd left Ireland a lifetime ago. One of them, Mrs. Collins from the Avenue, approached the coffin, nodded her head approvingly and muttered, "I've never seen you look so well Moya."

About the Author

Michael Cassidy was born in 1950 and raised in Limerick, Ireland. The date of his death has not yet been determined.

At nineteen, he talked his way onto a Dutch vessel in Dunmore East and worked his passage to Holland. He then joined the Dutch fishing fleet in the North Sea.

He has traveled extensively throughout his life. Apart from Ireland and Holland, he has lived in Canada, the United States, Costa Rica, and Brazil. He now lives on an island in the Philippines.

Some of his life experiences include being a failed but eventually successful father, a permanently unsuitable husband, a homeless street person, a hopeless drunk but subsequently a non-drinker, an uninterested insurance clerk, an incompetent deckhand, a decent stage actor, a dish washer, waiter, bartender, then restaurant owner, a non-practicing attorney, a newspaper owner and publisher, a TV presenter, a movie producer, a good friend, a bad enemy, a failed then successful businessman, and now, an author.

His next novel about the Irish immigrant experience in America will be published in 2018.

He may be contacted at irishauthormichaelcassidy@gmail.com.

Hello Reader,

Thank you for reading my book. I'd greatly appreciate if you would write a review on the retailer site of your choice.

FYI, I also narrated The Longfellah's Son on audio. It's available through most major audiobook retailers.

I'd enjoy hearing directly from you. My email address is irishauthormichaelcassidy@gmail.com.

I'm presently working on the sequel while living in the mountains on a Philippine island. The present working title is More Almost True Irish Stories. It is a collection of short stories that reflects on the Irish emigrant experience in America.

Thank you in advance for your review. I very much look forward to hearing from you.

Michael Cassidy